How To
Do Everything
And
Be Happy

D1150406

How To Do Everything And Be Happy

Your Easy-Peasy Guide to Creating Happiness

By Peter Jones

www.soundhaven.com

A SoundHaven Book

Text Copyright © Peter Jones 2011
Cover Design by Ellen V Wright ©

Published 2011, in Great Britain,
by SoundHaven Limited & Authors Online Ltd.
http://www.soundhaven.com
http://www.authorsonline.co.uk

All rights reserved. No part of this publication may be
reproduced, stored in a retrieval system, or transmitted in any form
or by any means, electronic, mechanical, photocopy, recording or
otherwise, without prior written permission of the copyright owner.
Nor can it be circulated in any form of binding or cover other than
that in which it is published and without similar condition including
this condition being imposed on a subsequent purchaser.
Please visit www.howtodoeverythingandbehappy.com
for contact details

ISBN 978-0-9568856-0-9

British Cataloguing Publication data:
A catalogue record of this book is available from

This boo

for your kindle

www.how

MORAY COUNCIL LIBRARIES & INFO.SERVICES	
20 33 78 60	
Askews & Holts	
158.1	

In memory of Kate,
her Big Theory of Everything,
and all the amazing things she taught me.
Love, as always,
Peter

Contents

To Begin With...

Once upon a time I got sold a dream: I would grow up big and strong, marry a blonde (my mother was convinced of this), have children of our own, and live happily ever after in a big house, whilst I held down a job as an astronaut. Or a train driver. Or a fireman. And this wasn't a 'maybe' - something to aspire to – this was my God given right. This is what was going to happen. All I had to do was wait.

Not that I was very good at waiting. I'm still not very good at waiting! I wanted this idyllic life now, at the tender age of six - or however old I was. I certainly didn't want to wait until *next week* or some other distant point in the future.

I must have told my parents this because they would smile and tell me not to be in such a rush. "Peter," they would say, "schooldays are the best days of your life."

I beg your pardon? Did you say "schooldays"? You mean the days I spend at school? The days I spend trudging to and from school in all sorts of weather? The days I spend sitting in boring classes? The days I spend dodging projectiles, hiding from the big kids, being chased, getting into fights? The days I spend looking at Melanie Jones or Karen Henderson from across the room – wishing either one was my girlfriend – sending them notes – watching them smooching with the same kids who'd taken my sandwiches earlier that day and thrown them over someone's fence – those days? Those are the best days I'm ever going to have?

Obviously they were mistaken. They had to be. When my parents' eyes glazed over and they talked fondly of 'schooldays' they must have been recalling the days of their own distant childhood, days sitting around camp fires outside the school mud hut, marking bits of slate with chalk whilst village elders told stories of dragons. Their schooldays were clearly a far cry from the mixture of humiliation, bullying and boredom that I endured. They had to be. Because if they weren't, for schooldays to be the 'best' days they would logically have to be followed by 'something worse.'

Then I got older, and things got worse.

Actually, that's not quite true. They didn't get any worse – not really – but they certainly didn't get much better, and they definitely got more complex.

'Work' turned out to be very similar to 'school' - different bullies, same rules, just as boring. And whereas I was given money in return for surrendering five days out of seven – more money than I'd ever dreamed possible – now there was a slew of people queuing up to take it away from me. What's more, all the things I'd looked forward to buying back when having a pay cheque seemed like the answer to everything turned out to cost roughly double the biggest number I could write on a single sheet of paper.

And then there were relationships. Just when I'd got classroom note passing down to a fine art, the game changed completely, and note passing wasn't going to cut it.

I could go on, but suffice it to say, the initial 'dream' seemed less and less likely. It was clear that I was never going to be an astronaut. Or a train driver. Or a fireman. It also seemed unlikely that I would ever live in a big house. Big houses needed big money. I was on small to medium money.

Two bedroom flat money. It wasn't a bad flat - a little pokey - but it certainly wasn't what I'd been promised.

And then on my thirty second birthday I finally realised there was also a distinct possibility that I might never ever find 'the blonde'.

This was a serious blow. Without the blonde I might never be married, I might never have children – and whilst I could probably cope without being married or having kids, or my blonde actually being a blonde ('female' and 'nice' was more than sufficient) I couldn't imagine being single for the rest of my days. That was unacceptable, and something had to be done.

So, for the first time in my life, I actually started to plan, and make lists, and take control of my own destiny. All the techniques you read in this book are basically an extension of the skills I had to develop to avoid a life of bachelorhood.

And you'll be pleased to know that I found the blonde. Took me a few more years, considerable effort on my part, and a somewhat unorthodox approach to dating, but I found her.

And we did marry.

And when she died in my arms three years later I was heartbroken.

It's a funny thing about losing someone you love. After the shock, the first thing you often feel is guilt. Every cross word, every nasty thought, every lie - they all come back to haunt you. And amongst the demons that were queuing up to torment me was the realisation that I wasn't happy. Even when my wife Kate had finally come along, I still wasn't happy.

Of course, there had been happy moments. Quite a lot of moments. And most of them were in the previous three years, and most of them were down to one person, but they were moments none the less. I wanted to be happy all the time. Not just occasionally. Not just for a moment. And for the second time in my life I decided to tackle a problem in the only way I knew how: by making plans, and lists, and taking control of my own destiny.

Welcome to 'How To Do Everything and Be Happy!'

If you're dissatisfied with your life, this book may be for you.

If you want to do something – anything – to increase the amount of happiness you feel, this book is probably for you.

And if you know how to use a pencil, if you own a diary, if you can make a list, if you're moderately organised, or could be if you had a good enough reason to be, then this book is definitely for you.

Now then, let me tell you about this dream that I have for you…

Why The Long Face?

"When you are unhappy, is there anything more maddening than to be told that you should be contented with your lot?"
Kathleen Thompson Norris, American novelist 1880-1966

General Unhappiness

It's 9am on a Monday morning. The sky is a threatening mix of greys. The wind has slammed every door in the house, taken the lid off the bin, thrown it down the street, and is now attempting to wrestle the trees to the ground. Meanwhile the rain is pounding against the window like it's trying to get in. It's not what you need right now, and none of it is doing anything to soothe your hangover. Or is it a headache? Either way, your head pounds as if your skull is slowly being crushed in a vice, and all you can do to ease the pain is rub your eyes - eyes that feel like someone rolled them in chalk dust whilst you slept. All you have to do is make it till lunchtime, and then - maybe - you can sneak out to the car and get your head down for 15 minutes.

Except that it's not Monday morning. It's Wednesday afternoon. On a balmy spring day. The sky's finally realised that when it comes to clouds, less is most definitely more. The only wind is a gentle breeze that carries the sounds of the children from the school opposite. It's only Monday morning inside your head.

But that's how you feel all the time. Or most of the time. Enough that it bugs you. Enough that you picked up a book on happiness.

And it's how I used to feel.

Right now, as I write this book, I estimate 92% of my life was spent being 'unhappy'[1]. Not in an 'active' way, just - you know - a bit pissed off with life. I had my share of moments where I stared at the cards life had dealt me and wondered how it was possible that there wasn't a single ace or picture card in my hand. I was 'a bit disappointed with it all'. There was a general lack of happiness in my days. I was un-happy.

In other words, I was, and very occasionally still am, pretty much like you, and most of the people we know. One of my closest friends once described it like this; "I'm not," he said, "living the life I would have chosen for myself."

So what's the cause?

Obviously there are numerous reasons. Therapists, psychologists and sociologists can probably carve them up and categorise them in numerous ways, but there are just three that seem right to me.

Let's take a closer look at General Unhappiness.

---

[1] My assistant asked me how on earth I came up with that figure. Then before I could answer she said, "You created a spreadsheet, didn't you!" I'm ashamed to admit it, but yes – I did.

Reason Number 1: Lousy Work/Life Balance

According to 'popular wisdom', no one lies on their death bed and thinks to themself, "I really wish I'd spent more time at work."

Or do they?

Perhaps, out there, there's some lucky fellow who has, or had, this amazing job, and they either did, or are likely to, lie on their death bed and wish they'd spent more time in the office. Who could that person be?

Let's consider some possible candidates:

CONTESTANT NUMBER 1:
TOM HANKS
A-LIST HOLLYWOOD ACTOR

You know, I bet even Mr Hanks gets fed up with being an A-list Hollywood Actor. It's not all glitz, you know. For one thing, there's the paparazzi, constantly hounding Britney Spears and ignoring Tom. What exactly does an A-list actor have to do to get his picture on the front of a few magazines these days? Where's the respect? What happened to the days when raw talent was enough to get you noticed? Nowadays those press guys are only interested in shoving a camera in your face when you're face down in a puddle of something foul.

Will Tom be wishing he spent more time at work when the time comes to visit the big awards ceremony in the sky? Not a chance.

CONTESTANT NUMBER 2:
BILL GATES
CREATOR OF MICROSOFT

Being the 2nd richest man on the planet[2] must be quite a buzz.

Thing is though, even if Bill decided to phone in sick, and to lie in bed for the rest of his life, he'd still be amongst the richest people that have ever lived – he doesn't actually have to *work* at it any more.

Now he might lie on his death bed and have regrets about Windows 95, Windows Vista, and Office 2007 - as well he should - but that would be a desire to atone for his crimes to humanity. In many ways those heinous errors of judgement may have actually been avoided if Bill had stayed at home once in a while. So when the time comes and Dr Watson walks into the room to tell Bill that there's been an unexpected error in his Life and it needs to Shut Down, will he wish he'd spent more time at the office?

No.

Next.

CONTESTANT NUMBER 3:
JULIO CASI AMOREO
WORLD'S GREATEST LOVER,
MALE ESCORT &
FIGMENT OF PETER JONES'S IMAGINATION

---

[2] at the time of writing

Maybe there's someone out there who gets paid to make love to the world's most fabulously gorgeous women. (What? It could happen!)

On his death bed in his villa, somewhere in southern Italy, surrounded by beautiful, grief stricken lovers, Julio looks around him and, as gentle breeze wafts in through the window and plays with his hair, he realises that even though he was managing three or four ladies, every day, for the past twenty years, he still failed to get to them all.

Maybe Julio will wish he'd worked more.

Well done. We thought of someone. Though we had to make him up. And you and I are probably in the minority for believing such a job can be described as 'work'.

It occurs to me that we probably need to take a moment to define what 'work' is. This isn't the dictionary definition, but it's one that feels right to me:

Work is:
➢ Anything you **have** to do (be that earning money, picking the kids up from school, paying bills, sorting through your post, chores, family commitments…)
➢ Doing whatever it is you *need* to do to sustain your life (earning money, robbing banks, living off the land…)

And, this being the case, here are some interesting things I've noticed about 'work':
➢ Most of us are conditioned to believe that we <u>must</u> work. (Sure, many of us *have* to work, to earn money for food, clothes, and to keep a home running – but the

conditioning is actually a belief that we <u>must</u> work, and that we're lazy, or stupid, or not pulling our weight if we don't.)

➢ Work tends to fill the space available.

➢ Some bright spark decided that the average working week should be five days out of seven. Five out of seven!

This being the case it's ridiculously easy to end up with a situation where work totally dominates your life. Where it's virtually the only thing you do during waking hours.

Try this simple exercise:

Taking no more than thirty seconds, think of three things you did in the last twenty four hours that don't fall under my definition of "work"?

Do that now, then turn the page.

So, you're done? What were your three things?
Were they…

 ➢ eating,
 ➢ watching TV,
 ➢ and sleeping?

If you had something better on your list (I'll let you off if you "went out for dinner") did it take you more than thirty seconds to come up with your list?

Now, I'm not suggesting for one moment that work isn't necessary and is somehow a *bad* thing. I'm not proposing that we eliminate work. Work is necessary. But for most people the balance of work and 'everything else' in their life is all wrong. And in many cases the 'everything else' lacks substance.

This being the case, there are three ways to improve your work-life balance:

Work less
Improve the 'something else'
Make work fun (which might involve changing the very nature of what 'work' is)

I've tried – and am still trying - all three approaches. Maybe you instinctively know that one or all of these might work for you, but try not to get fixated on that right now. Keep that thought in the back of your mind, or better still, *jot it on a piece of paper*. We'll come back to it later.

In the meantime let's move on to the second reason for General Unhappiness.

Reason Number 2: Lack of Control

Run down the following list and keep a count in your head of the number of times you say "yes, that applies to me."

1. Other people have a say in how your life works.
2. *Everyone* else gets a say in how your life works.
3. You feel powerless a lot of the time.
4. Everyone, and everything else, comes first.
5. You say things like, "I can't do {what I want}, because I've got to do…"
6. What you want (to do) is right at the bottom of your to-do list.
7. Your to-do list is mainly a list of items given to you by someone else.
8. You say things like, "Things will be much better when..."
9. This isn't the life you would have chosen for yourself.
10. You find yourself jealously protecting the half-an-hour you have to yourself each day ...
11. ... or the one night a week when you go to your evening class, club, pub etc.
12. You have secret friends, hobbies, lovers, possessions… anything, just something that you can call *yours*.

How did you score? I scored one, perhaps one and a half. A few years back I would have scored a nine, maybe even a ten.

Things were pretty miserable back then: I would get up really early in the morning just so I could be on my own. I would go to work an hour earlier than was strictly necessary, and I'd take the scenic route there. Once at work I'd count the hours till lunchtime, and then again till I could leave. Then I'd drive the long way home, a different route this time, with a certain amount of dread about what awaited me when I got in.

Once home I'd get cross if there was anything that needed my attention – something to fix, a phone call to make, or even post to open. I'd get cross if there was nothing for dinner. I'd get cross if I couldn't watch television (though I didn't care what was on). And I'd definitely get cross if I couldn't have a glass of wine. Particularly as I wanted two. And after all this crossness I'd go to bed. Ridiculously early.

My days would be spent impatiently waiting for the next 'bit', just so whatever I was currently doing would end.

I'd spend weekdays longing for the weekend, and the weekend longing for Monday morning.

And I spent hours and hours wishing. I made long secret lists of wishes: 'Things I would do someday...' Except someday never came. My only purpose in life was to make sure my body was where it was supposed to be at an allotted time. I was a prisoner inside my own existence.

And the really sad thing is, I wasn't the only one. My wife felt like that too. We were both slaves to a growing number of responsibilities that controlled our every waking hour.

So who was holding us to ransom? Who was pulling the strings? Who was the evil mastermind behind the wicked forces in our lives?

We were.

We let it happen. And it wasn't hard to do.

What's more, we thought it was a phase. A blip. Something to get through. Good times were just around the corner, and if they weren't, we still had the rest of our lives for things to get better.

And whilst that might be true for me, it wasn't for my wife.

If I could jump back in time and tell my younger self that I'd only be with Kate for three years and three months, and that those would be the very last moments she would have on this planet, I'd change everything. Right away.

In short: I'd have made every damn day count.

Let's get one thing straight here. You can't live every day as though it's your last. That's impractical. Stupid, even. But you can grab back the reins of your life, get back in the driving seat, and take back control. It's not easy. There'll be resistance. Lots of it. The majority of it from yourself. But my God, you'll feel better.

Now, you might be thinking, "Terrific! Another self-help book that wants to tell me how the unhappiness I feel is my fault! What a crock! Can I get a refund?"

Relax.

This book's being written by an Englishman, and as such it's finally time to start pointing the finger at others.

Reason Number 3: External Forces

Sometimes the thing that's making you unhappy is staring you right in the face. People might tell you that you need to relax more, calm down, try not to take things personally, roll with the punches, "make lemonade when life gives you lemons", but sometimes that's not going to cut it.

Sometimes, it isn't you.

Sometimes it really is *them*.

Let's take a look at who *they* are.

For me, 'Other People' have more power than anything else to drain my enthusiasm and suck the pleasure out of life.

It isn't always the people you think it would be either. Sure, the angry idiot who gestured at me from his car as he drove past took the edge off what might have been a pleasant drive home, but he's soon forgotten, and I can take solace in the fact that by the way he's driving he'll probably wrap his car around a tree in the not too distant future.

No, the people who really have the power to make me *really* unhappy are either people who I care about, or people who are, in some way, important in my life.

We all have them: The manager you don't get on with - one who seems intent on making your life a misery. The ex-partner you still have to see at family gatherings. Less extreme but just as soul destroying might be the moody work colleague you have to tip toe around. Or the aged relative who you love dearly, but has started to take you for granted.

Sometimes it isn't the interaction with these people, but the lack thereof. Like the client or a supplier who never returns your calls, never answers your emails, and is somehow never in the office when you 'pop by'. Or the friend or sibling who is so wrapped up in themselves that after an hour or so in their company you really begin to wonder whether all you are is some sort of audience.

Then there are the corporations, companies and government bodies that determine the structure in which we live. Rarely does a day go by when I haven't got to deal with some browbeaten representative from a corporation or organisation that really couldn't give two figs about whatever my plight might be.

Sometimes it feels as if these organisations must be run by people whose entire aim in life is to make as much money as possible, by any means, but without bringing the *slightest* bit of joy to anyone involved in the process. And having worked for a number of such organisations I can divulge that this is indeed the case.

That's just me, of course.

So in order to make this section a little more rounded I decided to conduct a quick poll by email with a view to coming up with half a dozen broad sub categories of what brings people down.

That may have been a mistake.

In the last two minutes I've been so overwhelmed with ranting emails that instead of depressing both you and myself, I'm just going to list a tiny extract of the items that made me smile or had me bouncing up and down in agreement.

External Forces – popular culprits

- Hormones
- Not getting enough sleep
- People who walk in front of me very, very slowly
- Being late for anything
- Not getting any sleep
- Rubbish pre recorded Call Centre messages – "We're experiencing a high volume of calls at the moment" – no you're not! This is the same volume of calls you've had for the past ten years! You just haven't got enough staff and you don't want to take my call!
- Loud, constant noise (e.g, the roadworks we've had outside my building since I started this job)
- Unfairness
- Making a mistake
- Losing out on a job
- "If your call is about something trivial, press 1. If your call is related to something else trivial, press 2. If your call is related to a trivial matter not related to the first two trivial matters press 3. If your call…"
- Clients who yell at me or get annoyed just because they can, when there's nothing I can do about it
- The UK winter (being dark at 4pm)
- Friends letting me down or losing touch with friends
- Family not 'understanding' me or saying something that makes me feel a bit low
- "Did you know you can check your balance or order a replacement card via our website…" Yes, I did! Stop

telling me this rubbish and put me through to a real
person!
➤ Having a fat day or a bad hair day (yes I am a girl)
➤ Being broke and worrying about money
➤ The January sales when I'm trying to save
➤ Getting stressed about 'my life'
➤ Family or friends being sick or ill, i.e. worrying about
them
➤ Not spending enough time with my family
➤ Not having a holiday
➤ Being lonely - stuck in the house
➤ Realising I haven't done anything fun for weeks
➤ Parking tickets or fines
➤ ANY kind of fine, e.g. bank fees
➤ Having to go to the doctor
➤ Paying for a coffee then finding that it's rubbish (same
goes with going out for a meal and it's bad food and
bad service)
➤ "I'm a state of the art automated telephone system.
Please tell me the nature of your problem." "I'm sorry,
I thought you said you have a frog in your bidet – is
that correct?"
➤ Reading bad news in the newspaper
➤ Thinking about climate change
➤ Other people littering
➤ Walking past homeless people
➤ Bad hairdos
➤ Boredom
➤ Mess, that I have to clean up

> ➢ Procrastination (makes me guilty, then consequently blue)

Doubtless you'll have your own items that you can add to that list[3]. The question is - what can you do about it? How can you reduce the power these things have over you?

In my opinion the first step is to recognise when there's a problem that needs addressing. This might seem obvious but in my experience it usually takes someone else, someone who we might be getting grumpy with, to say "Hey - what's bugging you?" before we finally face up to the fact that there's an external force in our life that's dragging us down.

Allow me to be that person right now, and ask the question: "What or who's bugging you?"

Got an answer?

Good. Write it down. Later in the book we'll talk about ways of developing and executing a plan to deal with that issue head on. In the meantime, I'd like to bolster your armour a little and discuss a few simple ways to limit the influence these situations have over you.

Beating the Blues

What follows are five bullet proof layers partly inspired by my friend Agent Sparkles[4] who created a 13 point *beat-the-blues* survival guide after a difficult period in her life

---

[3] Feel free to share them with me; visit the website at www.howtodoeverythingandbehappy.com

[4] She's a secret agent. I could tell you her real name, but then she'd have to kill you.

struggling with depression. You can find Agent Sparkles's list, unedited and in its entirety on the website at howtodoeverythingandbehappy.com - for now, however, here are five items that really work for me.

Bullet Proof Layer 1 – Put Your Pants On!
Every morning, before 9am, and regardless of what day of the week it is and whether you have any plans – *get out of bed.*

Get up, have a shower, get dressed, put on decent clothes. Do your make up, do your hair, shave your legs – or whatever your personal equivalent may be. This sends a strong message to your psyche that you're ready to face the day.

This is doubly important for people who work from home.

Bullet Proof Layer 2 – Eat Properly
After millions of years of shovelling food into our mouths it seems like we're only just beginning to realise that the old saying "you are what you eat" is actually true. Every single cell, every hair, every flake of dandruff, every tear, every bead of sweat, every inch of skin, muscle and bone, all of it was constructed by your body from something you (or your mother) ate.

This includes your brain.

If you have a habit of eating rubbish on a daily basis you'll end up with a brain that's not as able to cope with the stresses or strains of everyday life. That melon-sized lump of grey matter in your skull really is less efficient if it's been constructed out of crisps, burgers and chocolate bars!

Fortunately this is very easy to fix. Whilst cultivating a 'better diet' (i.e. lots of fresh fruit and vegetables whilst avoiding processed foods wherever possible) is just good sense, there are *specific* foods that are good for your brain.

Omega 3 fatty acids, for instance, directly affect your brain's ability to cope with stress, depression, concentration and memory. Study after study has shown that an increase of Omega 3 in your diet can make a huge, measurable difference to how you feel.

So where can you get your Omega 3? Flax seeds and walnuts are a good source, though you've got to eat a lot to notice a difference (crush them up beforehand to reduce the chances of them passing straight through you). A better source is oily fish (such as mackerel and salmon) because the fish has actually done much of the work, converting the fats into a form ready for your body to digest.

If you haven't got the time to start grilling fish once or twice a week there's always *supplements*. It's worth mentioning that there's research to suggest that you absorb far more Omega 3 from food than from supplements, but from personal experience I've found supplements to be an acceptable alternative – but remember, they're *supplements*, not meal alternatives. Nothing beats a balanced diet of three proper meals a day with plenty of fruit and veg.

Bullet Proof Layer 3 – Sleep
Almost everyone who came back to me with their list of External Forces sited tiredness or sleep deprivation as a cause of unhappiness. Which isn't surprising really. It's a rare person who can keep a positive upbeat attitude when they're walking around like a zombie.

So - go to bed at a reasonable hour, and go to sleep. This means if you're aiming to get up at 8am you probably need to be lying down, ready to sleep, by eleven.

If you're struggling with insomnia then an excellent book on the subject (written by a sleep doctor) is "Tired But Wired: How to Overcome Sleep Problems[5]" by Nerina Ramlakhan.

Bullet Proof Layer 4 - Daylight

First, the basics. Having got up in the morning (bullet proof layer 1) – open the curtains. A lack of sunshine can really drag you down. But do you know why?

All living organisms have an internal biological clock (of sorts) called a circadian rhythm. This internal process regulates a number of bodily functions and for most people their 'rhythm' is approximately a twenty four hour cycle. Approximately.

And there's the rub. Your cycle is only approximately the same length as a normal day. If it's a little on the short or long side (which it easily could be) it's possible for your circadian rhythm to become out of sync with your lifestyle, the effect of which is to leave you feeling like you're suffering from permanent jet-lag (because essentially that's exactly what jet-lag is). It's not uncommon to experience insomnia, acute tiredness, lethargy, anxiety, even depression.

Fortunately your body has a 'reset button'. If when you wake enough light reaches your eyes (or specifically a group of cells called ganglions) your circadian rhythm is reset.

---

[5] ISBN-13: 978-0285638778

Notice the *if* in that sentence. If you spend your days asleep, and your nights sitting in front of the TV or computer, your rhythm might actually fail to reset itself. For some people, one too many winter days has the same effect[6], and before you know it you feel as if you're stumbling through life with a head full of porridge, boxing with one hand tied behind your back.

That's not a good state to be in if you also have to deal with your evil boss, your interfering mother-in-law, that angry idiot from next door, or whoever it is that has the ability to press all your buttons - and if you're not getting enough daylight those buttons are fully exposed and there for the pressing.

Bullet Proof Layer 5 – Trust that 'Things Will Get Better'
In the words of my favourite quote:

EVERYTHING WILL BE ALRIGHT IN THE END.
IF IT'S NOT ALRIGHT,
IT'S NOT THE END.

---

[6] Commonly referred to as SAD (Seasonal Affected Disorder). SAD can be reversed, without drugs, pretty much overnight. My personal therapy of choice is a 'light box' to take the place of sunshine.

Doing Something About It

So, let's recap.

The top three reasons for General Unhappiness (according to me anyway) are:

Lousy work/life balance
Where the things you *have* to do dominate your life, and the things you'd *like* to do just aren't meaty enough, or you don't have enough of them, to 'balance' your life.

A general lack of control
Where you find yourself bouncing around the pinball machine of life, and you're not in control of the flippers.

External forces
Where you encounter people or situations that seem intent on taking your sunny smiley mood and crushing it into the ground.

Now, would you like to do something about it?

During the pages that follow I'll take you through practical steps to (re)organise your life so that you increasingly find yourself doing things that make you happy, and spending less time churning through the stuff that sucks the joy out of life.

You might be surprised to find that putting the smile back on your face won't necessarily involve identifying problem areas of your life and attempting to 'fix' or eliminate them. Happiness doesn't seem to work that way. And whilst it's useful to know why you're unhappy, oddly enough an absence of unhappiness isn't happiness.

That said, we are going to improve your work/life balance. We're also going to snatch back control of your life and put you back in the driving seat. And finally we will start redesigning your life so that those external influences either won't seem so influential, or won't be there at all.

This book's designed to get you started right away. We'll start with the easy stuff and build on it. If you work with me as we go through the various chapters you'll start feeling better about life within a few days, and better still as the weeks go by.

So, let's get started.

Making Time to be Happy

"If you have one eye on yesterday, and one eye on tomorrow,
you're going to be cockeyed today."
Anonymous

Boxing Day

For many years in my family Boxing Day, the 26th of
December, used to be a re-run of Christmas Day. Sometimes
the venue would change but there was always *another* roast
turkey dinner, *more* Christmas crackers, *more* party hats,
another Christmas pud, *more* mince pies and *once again* no
one would even touch the Christmas cake. When we were
very, very young there even used to be a second round of
present giving.

When my wife came along, Boxing Day became 'our'
day. We'd get up around midday, open a bottle of champagne,
play with our presents from the day before, roast chestnuts in
the oven, play silly board games, watch Christmas movies,
and eat posh nibbles. It was, quite simply, a fantastic day. Our
first Boxing Day together (before my wife was even my wife)
I even ended up proposing. That gives you some idea how
good Boxing Day made me feel about life, and there hasn't
been a Boxing Day since that hasn't given me that same inner
glow, that same joy for life. And I can speak with some
authority here because in the last four years I've celebrated
Boxing Day forty eight times.

That first Christmas after Kate passed away my mother, concerned for my welfare during the festive season, asked if I'd like to spend Boxing Day with them. It was a generous offer but, call me sentimental, I decided to spend it just as we always had.

I got up late, I opened a bottle of champagne, I sat in bed and browsed my collection of gifts from the previous day. Then I took the Brie from the fridge, a box of posh crackers (the edible kind) and worked my way through the whole lot whilst I sat in front of the telly and watched "The Santa Clause". A little later I emailed friends I'd been meaning to catch up with, and followed that with a walk down to Old Leigh. I looked out at the boats resting in the mud, and then I went home, wrote down some thoughts, and did some planning.

By the time I went to bed I felt like I'd had a week's holiday, and all I'd done was get out of bed and see how the day unfolded. It was such a good day that I caught myself wishing that Boxing Day happened a little more frequently than once a year, at which point I had the following crazy thought:

Why can't it?

What was to stop me replicating the same structure - or lack of structure - on any other day of the year?

Answer: nothing.

From that day on I decided to have a "Boxing Day" once a month. Once a month I'd get up with absolutely no plans whatsoever and see how the day unfolded. And that was almost four years ago.

There have been successful Boxing Days (in that I achieve that holiday feeling by the end of the day) and less successful Boxing Days (when I didn't), but there have never been *unsuccessful* Boxing Days (days when I somehow felt more stressed at the end of the day than the beginning). But of all the ideas I've had over the years, Boxing Day has been without a doubt one of the easiest to implement - which is why it's at the start of this book.

The Principles of Boxing Day

From here on, when I refer to Boxing Day, I'm referring to my Boxing Day, our Boxing Day, the one we are about to create in your life. Now whether or not you continue to spend the 26th of December as you have in previous years is entirely up to you, and whether you want to call your Boxing Day, 'Boxing Day' or 'Spontaneous Day' or 'Whatever I Want Day' or something else is equally up to you, but for the purposes of this book, Boxing Day will be the day when you give yourself permission to do whatever you feel like doing, within the realms of possibility, on the day itself.

Let's cover some basics here: Boxing Day isn't a 'day off', it's important to get that concept out of your head immediately. Boxing Day is a day when you get to live totally in the moment. And why is this important? Because living in the moment takes a lot less energy!

As adults we expend a huge amount of energy just juggling the day-to-day. Young children, on the other hand, don't. They live utterly in the moment and the job of structuring their day is handled by (hopefully) a responsible adult. Within the confines of whatever structure is imposed on them their day is totally driven by what they want to do, at that moment, and what opportunities exist. They don't have to expend any energy on thinking past the next few minutes, and as a result they seem to have bucketfuls of the stuff. You could probably power an entire city on half a dozen four year olds and a ball pool if you could just keep them in that ball pool long enough.

And four year olds never seem to suffer from that Monday morning feeling, they never seem to worry about how they're going to make it through the week, and they never pace themselves. They throw themselves at life, and when they run out of steam, they're done. Have you ever seen the way a four year old sleeps? They're so out of it you can pick them up without waking them.

Boxing Day is a little like being a four year old for a day. It releases you from thinking about the future or the past. For twenty four hours everything else is on hold. If you do Boxing Day properly you should feel like you've had a mini holiday – by the end of a Boxing Day you should feel rested, and energised, and happy.

So, let's reiterate how Boxing Day works in one concise sentence:

BOXING DAY IS DRIVEN BY THE MOMENT, THE HEART, AND THE OPPORTUNITY.

Re-read that last sentence because the success of your Boxing Days, should you choose to have them, relies heavily on how well you understand the concept and implement the principles. To boost your chances of success, however, there are some special Boxing Day rules.

Rules of Boxing Day

Rule Number 1: No Pre-Planning

You shouldn't plan your Boxing Day in advance. Everything you do on Boxing Day should be decided on the day, and determined by what you feel like doing, what's possible, and what opportunities present themselves.

Now you might say to me, "But I really need to finish decorating the spare room – taking a day to do that would be very useful." Well, fine. If you wake up on Boxing Day and you really feel like decorating the spare room – if that's the one thing that would really make your day – then go for it. Knock yourself out. Personally I hate decorating with a passion but there have been Boxing Days when I've decided to 'work', when that's the thing that I want to do more than any other choices that are available to me. The rule here is to not, under any circumstances, *plan in advance* to spend your Boxing Day up a ladder with a paint brush. If you know that spare room needs to be decorated then my advice to you is to take another day off to do that, and keep Boxing Day separate. And if decorating the spare room is really that important, write it down on a piece of paper and come back to it when we discuss Goals later in this book.

But then you might say to me that your wife/husband/significant other won't stomach the idea of you taking a day off 'to do nothing'. To which I would say, you're not going to do 'nothing'. You're going to do lots. You're just not going to plan it in advance, and you're not going to let anyone else determine what you choose to do.

Now having been married I appreciate that this might be *challenging*. So, one way to get buy-in from your significant other is to have a Boxing Day together or, better still, *individual* Boxing Days, albeit on the same day. This would avoid a day spent negotiating what the two of you are going to do – or, worse still, one partner dictating or submitting to the other – but I'll leave that for you to decide.

You might also say to me, "But I'd like to take the kids to this or that attraction and we need to book tickets in advance." Great. Jot that idea on a piece of paper and we'll come back to it in a few pages time when we discuss "Now Lists", but pre-planning a trip to an attraction isn't a valid Boxing Day activity. Waking up on Boxing Day and saying, "Hey, let's all go to the zoo," that's fine. Deciding to do it the day before and booking your tickets online – that's not allowed.

And stop stamping your feet on the floor and pulling that face. How old are you? Five? These are the rules and they're there for a reason.

Finally, you might whine, "But I can't afford all these days off! I only have x number of days off per year. Blah blah blah." Oh, for goodness sake! Then allocate one Saturday or Sunday per month to be your Boxing Day! There's no reason to start using up your holiday allocation.

Rule Number 2: Book Boxing Day in advance
This might seem to run contrary to rule number 1, but the only element of Boxing Day that should be pre-planned is deciding when your Boxing Day is going to take place.

If, like me, you use an electronic diary then I recommend you create a monthly Boxing Day appointment. Make it the 26th of each month if you like, especially if you intend to treat the official Boxing Day (the 26th of December) as a Boxing Day. In reality, it doesn't matter when your Boxing Day takes place, so long as it's *regular* and *booked in advance*.

You might have thought that given the spontaneous nature of Boxing Day activities it would make sense for Boxing Day itself to happen spontaneously – wait until you wake up one morning and if you're in a Boxing Day mood, declare that day Boxing Day.

There are two problems with this approach.

Firstly, if you're a workaholic, a 'busy' person, or you work at least 5 days a week and have commitments most weekends (i.e. someone like me), spontaneity might be something that you struggle with[7]. Therefore a spontaneous Boxing Day would inevitably involve cancelling whatever you had planned. Faced with a lot of last minute diary shuffling, a task that no one enjoys, it might be easier to be spontaneous another day. Pretty soon Spontaneous Boxing Day would become something that you intend to do, someday,

---

[7] My wife often complained that I wasn't spontaneous enough. In my defence I said that this was nonsense and that I loved being spontaneous, I just preferred to plan it in advance.

but keep putting off. "I'll have a Boxing Day tomorrow,"
you'll say. "There's just too much to be done today."

Secondly, if you're the total opposite of the person above
(How do you live? Seriously – how?) then there's an equally
good chance that you won't have *any* problems cancelling
work, or anything else you had planned. Assuming, of course,
that there was anything planned in the first place. Pretty soon
you'll be having Boxing Day on a fortnightly, weekly, twice
weekly, almost daily basis which will probably have two
knock on effects:

1.   the rest of your life won't work as the stuff that really
     needs to get done sits in the corner and gathers dust.
     Worst still, when you eventually get cut off by the
     electricity board you'll blame me and my stupid
     Boxing Day idea, and that simply won't do.
2.   Boxing Day will lose its potency. Yes, whilst you're
     sitting there in the dark, with the bailiffs knocking at
     the door, you'll cast your mind back to the day before,
     and the day before that, and the day before that, and
     realise that Boxing Day just ain't what it used to be - a
     week or so ago.

The only way to safeguard against these two scenarios is
to *book Boxing Day in advance*, and make an appointment
with yourself.

But, you might be saying, what if I desperately need a Boxing
Day? Or what if I'm due to have a Boxing Day but I'm not in
the mood, or it's just not convenient? Well, that's why you
need Rule Number 3.

Rule Number 3: You can move Boxing Day, but you can't
cancel it
It's a fact of life that no matter how much you try and
schedule your time "stuff happens". So if today was supposed
to be a Boxing Day but you've just had an echoey
conversation with your best friend who rang you from an
underground sewer after a freak manhole cover incident, open
your diary (planner/calendar/wall chart…), _reschedule_ Boxing
Day to another date, then throw a length of rope over your
shoulder, jump in your car and go rescue your friend.

Equally, should you wake up desperately in need of a
Boxing Day, open your diary (planner/calendar/wall chart…)
and see if you can _swap_ whatever you had planned for today
with your next scheduled Boxing Day.

Believe me, this strategy works well. I've been known to
postpone Boxing Days several weeks when Life is throwing
everything it can in my direction, and similarly I've been
known to have two Boxing Days within a few days of each
other if I've deemed it necessary. This rule allows me to
respond to the pushes and pulls of daily life whilst still getting
an average of 12 Boxing Days a year.

Of course, this rule, and rule number 2, are virtually
impossible if you don't have a mechanism to manage your
time.

Diaries

This is a good time to talk about the importance of having *and maintaining* a diary (and by diary I mean a calendar in which you write appointments, not a journal in which you ponder the meaning of life).

Time is quite possibly the most valuable commodity you have. Everything else can be bought with money, and money itself can be created, found, given, even stolen, but not time. You have the same number of hours in every day as everyone else. And whilst you have *some* influence over the number of those days you might have left believe me when I tell you that it doesn't matter how healthy or safety conscious you are, they can still be snatched away from you at any point.

You've probably heard it said that 'Time is Money'. But imagine if it was, and the hours and minutes of your life were somehow controlled by a Universal Bank of Time. What an austere organisation that would be.

Under their strict account usage terms, the UBT would actually mandate a compulsory daily *withdrawal* of 24 hours. The hours would be automatically transferred to you at the start of each day. However, you could never make a deposit. You could never put back what you didn't use – and unused hours would be taxed at 100%. Worse still, the Universal Bank of Time would steadfastly refuse to issue statements. There'd be no online banking with the UBT. You couldn't even get them to give you a balance, so you'd never be sure how much time you had left.

If real bank accounts worked this way you'd make sure you spent every penny of your daily withdrawal limit on something worthwhile. Pretty soon you'd probably start to plan your spending – you might even keep a book of items you wanted to spend your money on.

So why don't you do this with your time?

You don't expect to get in your car on Monday morning and have it drive you to work on its own, do you? No. You have to control the darn thing. And it's the same with your life. 'Taking control' comes in many guises but one of the simplest and most fundamental ways to take control of your life is to manage your time, and to do that:

YOU NEED A DIARY.

Here's what your diary needs to be able to do:
- ✓ It needs to be with you (*you*, not your partner), and preferably within arm's reach, at all times
- ✓ You need to be able to see a whole week at a glance
- ✓ You need to be able to put things in, take things out, and move stuff around, fairly easily

It would also be useful if it could do the following:
- ✓ Remind you of upcoming events
- ✓ Warn you about public bank holidays, birthdays, days such as "Mother's Day", changes to and from British Summer Time[8] etc.

---

[8] Daylight Saving Time

These days most people's mobile phones can be set up to do all that and more. But it's not the lack of diary options that stops people from using them, it's the fact that most people don't see the need for one. They're not very sexy. It's all a bit too much like hard work. So let me see if I can sell you some of the benefits of having a diary using real examples from my own life, when I was young and stupid.

Have you ever forgotten someone's birthday? Someone important? How did that feel? Did they give you a hard time about it? Did they get upset? Did they hurl things at you and, in a flurry of tears, accuse you of "not caring"? That wasn't true, was it – it was simply because your "current diary system" (i.e. keeping it all in your head) failed you dismally. Am I right? No? Ok, try this…

Have you ever missed an appointment? There you are, sitting on the couch, squinting at the TV, thanking your lucky stars you have an optician's appointment on – oh bugger, it was yesterday. You missed it. And why was that again?

Have you ever parked your car and noticed that the Road Tax expired last month? And when you went to renew your road tax you discovered that you no longer have a valid MOT certificate? Or insurance? Uh huh…

Have you ever arrived at work an hour early - or late - because the clocks changed at the weekend? And you didn't know? Feeling sheepish yet?

Do people phone you up to find out why you haven't turned up to that rehearsal / football match / band practice?

Does it ever seem like you spend your free days doing stuff for other people? Do you ever wonder why you agreed to do that in the first place? Do you ever wish you'd made time for yourself? Have you ever agreed to do something for two different people on the same day? How did it feel when you had to let one of them down?

Do you ever wonder where the time goes? Or how busy people fit it all in? Do you ever wish you could do more – for yourself, get a few things done, make things happen, finish decorating that room, take a day off, go to that concert, take a vacation, spend time with the kids, take a Boxing Day, be happier????

You need a diary!

Getting a Diary

There are some superb diary options out there. Until recently I was using Microsoft Outlook – I hated it with a passion, but it's what most of my clients use and it does the job, albeit in an annoying Microsoft kinda way.

I'm now using Google Calendar. Compared to Outlook, Google Calendar is, quite frankly, brilliant. Easy to use, free, and sophisticated enough that I can share various aspects of my calendar with trusted friends or work colleagues, and vice versa. My one and only gripe is that I have to use an internet browser to amend it, and more than once I've wished there was a proper Google Calendar application I could install on my machine[9], like the one I have on my iPod[10].

As you've probably guessed, I'm a diary nerd. And I like an excuse to play with technology. If you're a technophobe then an old fashioned Filofax would work just as well if you used a pencil and an eraser, and got into the habit of looking at it on a daily basis. Many, many years ago I used a Franklin planner and for a while that worked well. Then I moved on. "Upgraded", if you like.

In that respect, diaries are similar to computers. They don't seem like they're essential, but once you're using one

---

[9] Google does have an application you can download that allows you to view your diary on your computer when you're 'offline' (no internet connection) – but you can't amend your calendar, and you're still using a browser interface.

[10] CalenGoo is an excellent iPhone App that allows you to view and make changes to your Google Calendar, even when you're offline – there are alternatives.

you'll not only wonder how you coped before, but you'll need to upgrade it.

But let's just start with the basics. Let's get you using a diary and managing your time. Let's take action!

Action Points

Throughout this book there are various Action Points. These boxes serve as Stop signs. The idea is that you stop, address the action, and then continue.

Now clearly if you ignore the Action Point – the Stop Sign – it's unlikely that you'll be hit by a truck a moment later. Also I'm not going to pursue you through the proceeding pages, flag you down and issue you with a ticket and 3 points on your Amazon account. That's not going to happen.

Also, I've always been quite enthusiastic about 'ideas'. But whilst I like to collect and share ideas, I fully accept that you have just as much right to ignore them completely. I promise not to get annoyed with you for dismissing any suggestion (and these are only 'suggestions') I throw in your direction, if you promise to forgive me for being a little passionate, or teacher-ish.

That said, I'm assuming you bought this book because something in your head said "Hey – I *do* want to be happy" and way back on page three, four, something like that, we agreed (well, you read it and I didn't hear you object) that you couldn't achieve this aim without putting a little effort in. So as I'm writing the words, addressing the Action Points is your part of the deal.

With all that in mind here's the first Action Point of the book:

STOP! ACTION POINT!

Get yourself a diary

It can be a paper-based diary, the calendar on your phone, Outlook, Google Calendar, whatever. Just pick one.

Your diary should be:
- ✓ with you and within arm's reach, at all times
- ✓ able to show you a whole week at a glance
- ✓ able to let you put things in, take things out, and move stuff around fairly easily
- ✓ able to remind you of upcoming events
- ✓ able to warn you about public bank holidays, birthdays, days such as Mother's Day, changes to and from British Summer Time etc.

How To Use Your Diary

Hurrah! You have a diary. Fabulous. Now let's start using it.

You might think that's pretty straightforward but you'd be surprised – especially if you're a 'diary newbie' – how easy it is to screw things up. So here's my step-by-step guide:

1) Put ALL your appointments in it. Not just your appointment with your Physiotherapist or Family Planning clinic. Everything. Even the appointments you know you won't forget: your band rehearsals, your evening classes, even WORK. The only possible exception is **IF** you work a regular 5 day week (in which case put the times you're *not* at work in your diary – such as a vacation). If you don't work a five day week – if you work part-time, or shifts, or you're on a contract – put the work days in. Yes, it looks crowded! Now you know how busy you are.

2) Unless you have another system for this (one that actually works) add all birthdays and anniversaries, and potentially extra reminders a few days ahead of the real event (e.g. you might want an appointment entitled 'it's your wedding anniversary this time next week')[11].

---

[11] An excellent iPhone app that might make this gargantuan task easier is 'Occasions'. Occasions attempts to collate birthdays and anniversaries from the dates in your address book, as well as merging them with people you're friends with on Facebook etc. It'll then warn you about upcoming events. I use this 'warning' to decide whether or not these events get added to my diary.

3) Add bank holidays[12], Easter[13] (remember Easter moves around from one year to the next), Mother's Day[14], Father's Day[15], Christmas Day, Boxing Day (the real Boxing Day), Valentine's Day, and both days when they change the damn clocks[16] - in your diary. If your diary has a reminder function I recommend you set it to remind you several *days* in advance. Yes, days. Mine is set to 10 days (and the day itself). Birthdays are set to one month. There's no point in getting a reminder about an important birthday or anniversary on the actual day itself - not if you need to get a card and a gift (what d'you mean you always buy the card and gift on the day?)

4) Add your own birthday. You'll be surprised how many years I agreed to work on my own bloody birthday!

5) Delicate one, this one – you may wish to add your menstrual cycle, or the cycle of someone you're close to, to your diary. I'm just putting the idea out there. Moving on…

6) Start checking your diary regularly. How regularly? At least every day (set yourself an alarm if you have to until you get into the habit). You'll be surprised how often you discover an appointment you'd forgotten about. If your diary only allows you to see one day at a time (which is daft – ideally you want to be able to see the whole week in

---

[12] http://www.bankholidayinfo.com/

[13] http://www.wheniseastersunday.com/

[14] http://www.ukbankholidaydates.co.uk/mothering_sunday.html

[15] In the UK Father's Day is the third Sunday in June.

[16] http://www.whendotheclockschange.com/

one view) then don't just look at today - have a quick look at tomorrow, and the day after, and the day after that.

7) *Before you agree to anything* check your diary again. If the date's free enter the new appointment. If it's not, decline the appointment, or shuffle stuff around so you can make it.

8) **Do not agree to an appointment if you don't have your diary handy.** Here's how you avoid doing that – you say the following amazing magical phrase:
"Let me check my diary and get back to you."
See how easy that was?

9) Beware people who say, "What are you doing on...?" It seems like an innocent enough question, and - puffed up with pride in your newly organised life - it'll have you reaching for your diary and revealing to the other person that you're 'free'. Which then makes it virtually impossible to turn down their request to babysit their pet python. Even if you are busy you'll find yourself negotiating over whether what you have planned is more or less important than Percy the Python's happiness and well-being. The correct answer to "What are you doing on...?" is "Why do you ask?"

10) When agreeing to an appointment check the day before and the day after (so that you don't agree to "climb a mountain" the day after you "swim the channel").

11) When you add an appointment consider adding supporting appointments. Have you just accepted an invitation to a party? Great. Is it a posh do? Do you need your suit dry cleaned? Will you need a hat? Do you need a present? A card? A partner? Make appointments with yourself on

various days before the party to sort out all these things, along with an appointment (with yourself) to get ready for the party, and to journey to the party itself. Seriously. You'll thank me later. Oh, and book out the day after the party to "recover".

12) Take your diary with you <u>EVERYWHERE</u>. When you leave the house and you check you have your keys, check you have your diary.

13) And finally – make an appointment every month for a Boxing Day

STOP! ACTION POINT!

Pre-book your Boxing Days

Now that you have your diary, why not create a regular appointment with yourself for Boxing Day? I recommend you start with one a month – maybe on the 26th – always remembering that you can shuffle them about if they're not convenient.

Remember the principle of Boxing Day:

BOXING DAY IS DRIVEN BY THE MOMENT, THE HEART, AND THE OPPORTUNITY

And remember the Boxing Day Rules:
1. No pre-planning
2. Book Boxing Day in advance
   (which you've just done)
3. You can move Boxing Day but you can't cancel it

Potential Boxing Day Problems

I can't promise they'll have the same effect on you but Boxing Days have had a profound effect on my life; that simple one day a month has the power to restore my flagging enthusiasm for life in the way that so many exotic vacations in the past have utterly failed to.

That said, not every Boxing Day has been a rip-roaring success. Most of the time that's just because life's like that, but I've also discovered that Boxing Day has enemies that like to skulk around in the shadows, waiting for their chance to mess things up.

Fortunately, my suffering doesn't need to be your suffering. Here's the spotters guide to common Boxing Day problems.

Too many Boxing Days - Not enough Boxing Days
So, if one Boxing Day a month can work such magic, surely two Boxing Days a month would be twice as good, right?

Apparently not.

Believe me, I've tried.

For reasons that I've never really understood, too many Boxing Days actually reduces their effectiveness. They cease to be 'special' - and being 'special' is possibly what makes them work so well.

One Boxing Day a month seems just about right. Two just doesn't work.

However, this said, there's a chance that it might be different for different people. Unfortunately, even though I invented Boxing Day (or reinvented it... whatever...) I've only

myself to experiment on. Therefore I encourage you to
conduct your own experiments on yourself. If you feel you
need more, squeeze an extra one in and see if it works. If on
the other hand your Boxing Days start to feel more like a
boring Sunday afternoon than a week in a five star hotel, or if
you end up with a Boxing Day backlog (i.e. you postpone so
many that you actually start to have more than one "in the
bank") well, chances are you're having too many.

Boxing Day Boredom – or not knowing what to do
Ideally here's how Boxing Day should work. You wake up.
You ask yourself what you fancy doing at that precise
moment. And then you go and do that thing. And when you've
done that, or you've had enough of whatever it is, you go do
something else. Easy?

Well - not necessarily.

Once you've had a few Boxing Days it becomes
surprisingly difficult to keep your Boxing Days totally
spontaneous. I got into a bad habit of always having a bottle
of champagne, and always making a truck load of flapjacks.
Not only was this a tad expensive, but it was also a little
samey. Eventually Boxing Day started to lose its magical
powers.

Having got myself into this boozy, flapjacky rut, I
actually found it quite difficult to dig myself out. I ended up
creating a handful of tools to help me keep Boxing Day fresh
and, err, sober. Here then are some top tips should you find
yourself in a similar situation:

1) *Start Boxing Day from the moment you open your eyes* –
   Try and break from your normal daily routine from the
   moment you wake up. A couple of times I've come
   downstairs and as I've reached for the milk in the fridge
   I've seen those eggs, sitting there, quietly going off, and
   thought to myself – sod it – let's cook breakfast. And other
   times, as I opened the cupboard to take out the Weetabix,
   I've noticed a kilo bag of oats and thought to myself, "You
   know, what I really fancy right now are flapjacks."

2) *Perform the Boxing Day Dance* – Flushed with the
   success of the first Boxing Day (which you'll remember
   was an accident) I was quite excited when, having made
   an appointment with myself, it was time to have the
   second one. I was so excited that I danced round the flat in
   my dressing gown making up a silly Boxing Day song as I
   went, much to the bemusement of my cat. Strange thing is
   though, I've since found that if I'm having a Boxing Day
   which feels a little flat, a few bars of my Boxing Day song
   will be all I need to get the Boxing Day juices flowing.
   (No you can't hear my Boxing Day song – make up your
   own!)

3) *Do the first thing that comes to mind* – Sometimes it's
   difficult to decide what to do with your Boxing Day
   because you're over thinking it. If you're struggling to feel
   inspired, stop, and ask yourself "What do I want to do
   RIGHT NOW?" The thing that comes to mind, usually
   before you've even finished the sentence, is very possibly
   the thing you should do. It doesn't matter how silly it may
   seem, or how simple – if it can be done, now, and you like
   the idea – do it!

4) *You can work* – Working on Boxing Day is a completely legitimate exercise if that's what you really want to do. And let's broaden the definition of work to include any activity that you might not consider typically "fun". Decorating, for instance. Balancing your cheque book. Filling out an application form. Don't put yourself under pressure to fill your Boxing Day with "fun" activities. If it's what you want to do (*want* to do – not *need* to do) then it's a legitimate Boxing Day activity. For instance, I am writing this paragraph on Boxing Day! That's the absolute truth, and I can honestly say that right now, given the moment, the opportunities available to me, and how I feel, writing this is what I *really* want to do. (That said, I drove an hour and a half to Cambridge, and found myself the trendiest independent coffee shop to act as my writing venue. You get the idea.)

5) *Make a list* – Pre-planning Boxing Day is <u>utterly</u> forbidden, but if you're a planner at heart (as I am), there's nothing to say you can't do a little brainstorming at the start of the day. If I don't wake up and feel instantly inspired I often grab a piece of paper (rather than sit at my computer) and jot down ideas – things that I *could* do. I try and write my ideas all over the page and at weird angles so that it's as un-list like as possible (otherwise I might be tempted to start at the top and work through the items). And then, when I've finished brainstorming, quite often I'll toss the list to one side and do something entirely different.

6) *You can be dull* – If you want to do nothing but sit on the sofa and watch TV, or go back to bed, or read a magazine

cover to cover, or play computer games, that's perfectly acceptable. If it's been a while since your last Boxing Day (perhaps you had to postpone it) then maybe this is the first opportunity you've had in a while to rest. So do it. Rest. However, I encourage you to rest *with gusto* – if you want to go back to bed, put your PJs back on, close the curtains, put on some soothing music, maybe download some "ocean sounds" to your iPod, sprinkle lavender on your pillow – really go for it! If you want to watch TV, grab some snacks, then sit down and watch an entire season of Lost, or 24, or the Gilmore Girls, or Doctor Who, or whatever floats your boat.

Towards the back of this book, under the section 'Putting It All Together', you'll find an example of what a typical Boxing Day looks like (for me).

Pre-Planning your Boxing Day
No, no, no, no, and a thousand times no!

People ambush your Boxing Day
"What you up to today?" asks a friend.
  "I'm having a Boxing Day," you reply.
  That's not what they'll hear, of course. Somehow the words will get scrambled somewhere between leaving your mouth and entering their ears, and what they'll hear is: "I'm doing nothing."
  Which is why they suddenly invite themselves over, or ask if you'd like to help them paint their lounge, out of some

misguided notion that they're somehow enhancing your day
and you'd otherwise be sitting there bored out of your mind.

Bang goes Boxing Day.

It's a little like finding a tranquil picturesque location,
then sitting down to do a water colour painting, only to have
the person next to you reach over and start filling in bits you
haven't done yet. But can you tell them this? No. Of course
not.

There's only one solution to this problem. And it's a
matter of 'prevention' rather than 'cure' - keep your Boxing
Day SECRET, and when asked, tell people (including friends
- especially friends!) that you're doing something else!

Too busy to have a Boxing Day

There are two types of 'I don't have the time {for Boxing
Day}' people – those that don't have the time, and those that
think they don't have the time. Let's find out which type you
are.

Answer this simple question:

DO YOU HAVE AN APPOINTMENT DIARY
AND
DO YOU USE IT?

If you haven't answered yes to both parts of that question,
chances are you're one of the people who only _think_ that
they're busy. What you're calling 'busy' is in fact 'chaos'.

I'm not kidding about this: diaries really are _that_
important. Where were you when we covered this a few pages
back?

Go get a diary, start using it, then come back here.
The rest of you can turn the page.

So you're back. Good. Now hand me that diary and let's have a look.

Hmmm. I see. Well, you're right. You do appear to have a very busy schedule. Every single moment is indeed booked out for something. That'll be why you have that smug 'told you so' look on your face that's just crying out for a smack.

But wait - what's this appointment here? Every Sunday?

"That's when I go to see my mother," you say.

"Every Sunday?"

"Well, yes."

"Could you not skip it one week?"

"Not really."

"Why?"

"Because she expects me!"

"So tell her you can't make it one week!"

"I couldn't do that," you say.

"Why not?"

"Because she's my mother."

"Ok, but what about this Sunday? This Sunday you're not seeing your mother. This says 'work'."

"Well yes," you reply "there's this big project we're finishing up, and my boss really needs me – and besides, it's overtime..."

"So it's ok to cancel your mother if there's overtime up for grabs?"

"Well, we're really busy right now -"

"And your mother's ok with that?"

"Well, it's work – it's important."

"And you're not important?"

"Sorry?"

"I said: 'You're not important?'"

"Well, of course I am, I suppose -"

"You suppose?"

"Look, I can't cancel my mother, not to spend a day by myself-"

"Because you're not important?"

"Well, err-"

"Well?"

It's not that you're too busy, it's that you're putting everyone and everything before you and your happiness! You have, in effect, trained yourself - yes, *trained yourself* - to believe that when it comes to <u>your</u> time, and <u>your</u> life, everyone else gets to say how you spend it.

You *need* to stop that.

Of course, that's easier said than done. From birth we're encouraged by others to take on that 'training'. Eventually we might even convince ourselves that these habits of selflessness/martyrdom/workaholism are a good thing. We say to ourselves, "I must be a good person, I put everyone else first – yay me." Those that don't adopt a similar saintly attitude - and you can probably think of someone off the top of your head - can, on occasion, come across as a little self-centred or selfish. Maybe more than a little. And maybe not as occasionally as you'd like. Thank God you're not like that.

I bet they're happier though.

Now I'm not suggesting for one minute that you become like them, but accepting that you've created a habit of surrendering your time without question, and becoming aware of that habit, will give you the opportunity to say "no" and gradually regain control of your life. It'll feel uncomfortable at first. It may even feel wrong. At some point you'll upset someone. Maybe several someones. And that'll make you feel guilty. But these things will pass. With practice it'll become easier - it'll start to make sense - and the people around, those that care about you, will, eventually, adjust to the 'new you'.

So – let's start now - go tell your mother that you won't make it next week, or your boss that you can't come in on Sunday.

People who REALLY don't have enough time for Boxing Day
"Dear Mr Jones,

I recently purchased your book 'How To Do Everything And Be Happy' – and today I stopped reading it.

How dare you suggest that I am not really busy. There are those amongst us who are lucky if we can claw back five minutes from the day to spend doing what we want!

I am a single mother with two children and an elderly sick relative who needs my constant attention. When my day finally ends I sometimes spend a few minutes reading when I should probably be sleeping. This is the only time I get to myself, and I do not appreciate being told by you, a single man, that I'm not really busy.

You're right – I don't own a diary, but this is because I don't need to own a diary - every single day is exactly the same! And yes, you're right, everybody else does get to say how I spend my time - everybody else, as you quite rightly said, does come before me and my happiness. I don't like it, but that's how the world is, so you can take your book and shove it somewhere uncomfortable.

Yours sincerely,

Very Cross Person"

"Dear Very Cross Person,

I sympathise. I really do.

Much as this is a self-help book I don't have all the answers. I only wish I did. And the answers that I do have aren't necessarily easy to achieve, or right for everyone. I've never said they are.

Though I've never been in your situation I can appreciate how challenging it must be.

I know too that raising kids isn't just about getting the 'must dos' out of the way – I realise the importance of enabling your children to pursue their own activities and dreams whenever possible. For years my mother ferried me to and from cubs, scouts, drama club, youth club, swimming club... the list goes on.

Of all these activities swimming was a favourite. By the time I was in my early teens I was working on my survival badges. I'd spend evenings jumping in and out of swimming pools, fully clothed, picking up bricks from the bottom of the pool and taking it in turns to 'rescue' my fellow swimming club members. When the evening ended I'd present my mother with a bag full of sopping wet clothes without a second thought as to what she was going to do with them.

Whilst I was utterly guilty of taking my mother for granted, I was none the less learning some important skills. And though I've never had to rescue bricks or people, or inflate my trouser bottoms into a floatation device, or give anyone the kiss of life, there is one swimming survival concept that has stayed with me my whole life. We were always taught that when rescuing a drowning person, if the drownee begins to thrash or struggle, such that your attempts at rescue are being compromised, you need to push them away – just for a moment – just until you regain control, and you're able to resume your rescue.

Whilst finding an entire day to call your own might be impossible right now, it is, nonetheless, vital to look after yourself. I sincerely believe you need to find a way to push 'them' away – just for a few moments – and regain control of your life. Not just for your own sanity, but because you'll be no use to them if you drown.

Take care
Sincerely
Peter Jones"

General Boxing Day Failure
So you've had your Boxing Day – you obeyed all the rules, you took the advice above, and somehow it didn't rock your boat. Maybe it was a little dull. Maybe you sat down in the morning, thought of all the things you'd REALLY like to do and realised that due to a lack of something essential (money, opportunities, partners, super human powers, Brad and/or Angelina, whatever) all your ideas were impossible.

This can happen. It's happened to me, and when I came to analyse it (because sadly that's the sort of thing I do) I reached the conclusion that Boxing Days are great ... but they're not the whole answer.

Well, of course they're not! If they were then this would be the end of the book! And it's really just the beginning. Hold on to your hat because we've just gotten started!

Doing Those Things You Always Wanted To Do

"In the end, it's not going to matter how many breaths you took, but how many moments took your breath away."
Shing Xiong

So, how do you feel? Happier? How's Boxing Day working out for you?

Of course I realise that you've probably only just turned the page and you're yet to make your first Boxing Day appointment, let alone enjoy the experience, but I hope at the very least you're enjoying the book. You're still reading it - I'll take that as a good sign.

Onwards then.

Do you like movies?

The Bucket List

In 2007 Morgan Freeman and Jack Nicholson starred in a film called "The Bucket List". These two great actors play terminally ill gentlemen who share a hospital room. With only weeks to live the two characters write a list of things they want to experience before they "kick the bucket" – they call it their "bucket list" – and set about trying to complete each one.

Here's the list they came up with:

- Witness something truly majestic

- Help a complete stranger for the good
- Laugh till I cry
- Drive a Shelby Mustang
- Kiss the most beautiful girl in the world
- Get a tattoo
- Skydiving
- Visit Stonehenge
- Spend a week at the Louvre
- See Rome
- Dinner at La Chevre d'Or
- See the Pyramids
- Get back in touch
- Visit the Taj Mahal
- Hong Kong
- Victoria Falls
- Go on a safari
- Drive a motorcycle on the Great Wall of China
- Sit on the Great Egyptian Pyramids
- Find the joy in your life

It's a great movie. And it really makes you think: what would you do if someone gave you only six weeks to live?

Personally, if someone gave me six weeks to live I'd be a basket case by the end of the first afternoon! Assuming I could get my head round the shocking news, drawing up that list of experiences for my *final six weeks* would be like telling myself a thousand times over that I'd wasted the previous X number of years. And completing the items on my list would only serve to remind me of my dwindling mortality.

Basically - it's the stuff of nightmares.

I'd much rather be in a position whereby, having been given the awful news, I could take solace in the fact that I'd *already* had a life full of exciting, fun and interesting experiences. And were someone to hand me a legal pad and a pen I'd much rather struggle to think of anything I hadn't already experienced at some point in my life.

Of course, given that most of us have very little idea how many days we actually have left, for the above to be true I'd have to do something it about it, well… today! Now! I'd have to grab a pen (You do have one handy, don't you?) and start jotting down all those things that I want to experience, and then damn well set about doing them as soon as possible.

Guess what this section of the book's all about?

Creating a 'Live Life Now' List

Firstly, let's dispense with the term Bucket List. That's not what we're creating here. We don't want to be sitting in a hospital bed thinking of all the things we never did. What we want is to Live Life Now. So that's what we're going to call it. A 'Live Life Now' list – or a 'Now List' for short.

Writing a Now List is pretty straightforward. If you're a bit of a traditionalist – "retro" as the cool kids call it – take out a sheet of paper, write Now List at the top, then put it somewhere you'll find it again without a lot of searching.

If you're a little more tech savvy, I encourage you to create an empty document on your computer and/or phone and save it as "Now List".

Notice that all we're doing here is creating a *blank* document, and labelling it. If you can already think of items you want on your Now List then go ahead and write them down, but it's just as likely that you can't think of anything, or the one or two items you have seem a little lame. That's because all the things that *should* make your list are locked within your memory. They're the moments when you declared – either out loud or in your head – "I've always wanted to do that," right before you forgot all about it.

That's not going to happen again.

Next time someone tells you that they've just come back from a six month round the world trip, or someone asks you to sponsor them in the London Marathon, or you drive past that building you've always wanted to go inside, or your favourite band is advertising their next world tour, or a hot air balloon floats over your house – and you find yourself thinking, "Wow – I'd really love to…" – THAT'S the moment you're going to jot down a reminder and add that item to your Now List.

It's important then to *create an empty list now*, ready and waiting for your next "I'd really love to do that" moment. Trust me - don't wait until you have a Now List item. That doesn't seem to work. And how do I know that? Because that's exactly what I did! But once the list had been created ideas started coming thick and fast.

Save yourself some time – create the Now List, now.

STOP! ACTION POINT!

Create an empty Now List.

Whether you choose to maintain an electronic list, or a paper one, go and create your Now List now, ready for the next time you say "I'd really love to…"

What should be on the list – and what shouldn't

Anything you write on your list should be an answer to the following question:

**WHAT WOULD I LIKE TO EXPERIENCE
(BEFORE I DIE)?**

The key word there is *experience*. This isn't some sort of to-do list of things you have to get done before you check out. So items like "make sure the kids are taken care of", or "pay off the mortgage," or "give my stash of Doctor Who comics to my nephew" have no place on your Now List.

Similarly this isn't a list of goals or personal milestones. So whilst you might want to 'write a best-selling novel,' or 'learn to play the saxophone,' or 'get married,' or 'patch things up with your Aunt' all before you run out of days, they're a little bigger than mere experiences. They're all fabulous - and if any of these things resonate with you then you should definitely consider doing them, but - without wanting to get ahead of ourselves - jot them down and we'll come back to them in the next section.

Your Now List should be made up of experiences that theoretically you could do today, if money, time, pre-planning, and your diary allowed. In other words, your Now List is for all those things you couldn't do on a Boxing Day because they require some pre-planning.

So for example, here's my Now List:

- Take a narrow boat through Birmingham
- Own or have access to a boat

- Get close to monkeys
- Get close to dolphins
- Make Mum's Treacle Tart
- Visit the Minack Theatre
- Move to a warmer climate
- Have dinner with Imogen Heap
- Work with Stephen Moffat
- Rome!
- Go back to Sorrento
- Visit Hong Kong
- Go round the world (in a westerly direction)
- Visit the Cook Islands
- Play a part in The Importance of Being Earnest

Now, there are a couple of items on my list that bend the rules a little. 'Having access to a boat', and 'moving to a warmer climate', these are both items that might improve the quality of my life, but they're stretching the term 'experiences' – particularly 'moving to a warmer climate'.

To be true Now List items I could re-write them as follows:

- Go on boat trips (see my house from the Estuary)
- Enjoy the experience of living in a warmer climate

That last one's still a bit of a stretch, isn't it?

Though it's interesting how a little re-wording puts a different spin on things; 'enjoying the experience' doesn't sound quite as permanent as 'move to a warmer climate'. The latter is all about selling up and moving out, whereas the former might just be about renting a place abroad during the winter time.

Now if, having peeked at my list, you're already getting ideas or you want to pinch some of mine, well what are you reading this for? Go – add those items to your list! Do it now!

Categorising your Now List

The problem with the underlying Now List question ("What would you like to experience before you die?") is that it's totally overwhelming. It's a little like when someone asks you to tell them a joke – every joke you've ever heard momentarily disappears from your head. Even really funny people struggle to think of anything to say[17].

But if we break the 'before you die' question into sub questions, they become 'smaller', and easier to answer.

For instance, aside from the obvious 'What places would you like to visit (before you die)?' are there any bands you'd like to hear play? Or plays you'd like to see or be in? Effectively what we're doing here is breaking your Now List into categories which will help to generate ideas AND make the list easier to manage.

Two of my favourite categories are:

➢ Distant Dreams (for items that seem utterly ludicrous right now – e.g. walk on the moon)
➢ Food I'd really like to try

---

[17] Here's a good one: two fish in a tank, one says to the other, "How d'you drive this thing?"

These are only suggestions. If you're not a foodie, forget about the food category. If you're a sporty person, or a musical person, you might like to create categories for those. It really doesn't matter. But the more categories your Now List has, the easier it gets to think of items you want on it.

With categories, my list looks like this:

Time Sensitive
- Take a narrow boat through Birmingham
- Visit the Minack Theatre
- See Imogen Heap. Again.
- Go to a Bill Bailey gig

Animal Magic
- Get close to monkeys
- Get close to big cats
- Get close to dolphins

Places I'd like to Visit
- Rome!
- Go back to Sorrento
- Visit Hong Kong
- Go round the world (in a westerly direction)
- Visit the Cook Islands

Distant Dreams
- Have dinner with Imogen Heap
- Work with Stephen Moffat
- And Richard Curtis

Food I'd really like to try
- Make Mum's Treacle Tart
- Try deep fried crickets or some other insect (from the night time food market in Beijing)

Other
- Go on boat trips (see my house from the Estuary)
- Enjoy the experience of living in a warmer climate
- Play a part in The Importance of Being Earnest

'Time Sensitive' is a useful category to have. It forces you to think of all the things you'd like to do which are anchored to a particular point in history or season. The 2012 Olympics, for instance; I'm pretty sure it'll be over by 2013. And a narrow boat holiday through the centre of Birmingham in the middle of January might be a little grim. That's definitely a summer activity.

Notice how a few new items have found their way onto my list. The Treacle Tart item looked quite lonely sitting on its own in the food category, which is when I remembered something else that I've always wanted to eat – deep fried crickets! That's the power of categories.

Remember, your Now List items don't have to be hugely impressive. My brother turned his nose up when he discovered that seeing Imogen Heap is on my list. "That," he said, "is not really a Now List item." Which brings me to a very, very important point:

IT'S <u>YOUR</u> LIST.

It's your happiness you're planning here. If other people don't like the items on your list tell them to make their own! Seeing Imogen Heap is a big deal for me. Therefore it makes the list. Some people absolutely love movies. Those folks might start creating a list of films they must see 'before they die' and who are we to tell them that they can't do that? My friend Tina has a cupboard full of board games that she could never coax any of her family to sit down and play. Consequently, 'organise a games evening' went on her Now List[18].

Finally, a word about the 'other' category. Generally speaking I'm not a big fan of categories called 'other' or 'miscellaneous'. They very quickly become a dumping ground for items that should have a category of their own - but when it comes to Now Lists this can be a good thing. It'll encourage your imagination to dream up stuff that doesn't fit under the other categories you've created. As soon as your 'other' category has two or more items that look like they could team up and form a category of their own go ahead and do that.

Time, I think, for some action:

---

[18] It took place back in February. A hilarious evening! I'm thinking of stealing the idea and putting it on my list.

STOP! ACTION POINT!

Create Now List categories

Aside from the obvious 'places you'd like to visit' category, and an 'other' category, think of categories that'll help you generate ideas for your Now List. You might use some or all of the following:

Places I'd like to visit
Food I'd like to try
People I'd like to meet
Distant Dreams
Animal Magic
Bands I'd like to see
Books I really want to read
Sports I want to master
Time Sensitive
Other

Making Your Now List 'Happen'

So, you have your Now List – what now?

This might seem like a daft question. Obviously the answer is "start working through it" – but – if you're like me, you might go for the popular second choice: "put it in a drawer (virtual or otherwise) and ignore it."

That's what I did with my list for the first year. Which meant that from the very first moment I decided to create a Now List, to the day I started to do something about it was *18 months*. A year and a half of my life had rolled by when I could have visited several amazing places or eaten many strange and wonderful things.

So, you might ask, why did it take me so long?

It's hard to say. Maybe I took a look at the list and realised that most of the items were going to take some planning, or money, or time, or something else I didn't have at that exact moment.

Maybe I was afraid – after all, I hate travelling on my own and my list does have quite a few places that I'd like to visit. But not on my own.

Maybe I had a deep rooted psychological desire to maintain the status quo of my life and the Now List threatened that by representing *change*. Do the items on my Now List and I might, for a moment, *feel happier*. Once happier, I might be driven to change more things in my life. Where would it all end?!

Who knows. Who cares! The point is, the list was locked away and as such it was a waste. A waste of paper, a waste of time, and a waste of potential happiness.

Which is why I created Now List Day.

Now List Day

Welcome to your Now List Day. A day, once a month, where one of two things will happen:

1. You will enjoy an item on your Now List, or
2. You will work through your Now List and take whatever actions necessary to make your Now List items a reality.

So first, go back to your diary (You do have a diary, don't you? Let's not get started on that again ...) and book out one day a month for a Now List day.

Those of you who struggled to find one day a month for Boxing Day will be bouncing off the walls right now at the thought of clawing back a few hours to spend on your Now List, so I'll cut you a deal: if you really can't find a whole day then allocate a couple of Now List evenings, mornings, or lunchtimes. Whatever works for you. Just regular slots. Now clearly it's going to be difficult to climb Mount Everest during your lunch hour, or visit The Seven Wonders of the World, or play with Eric Clapton at Wembley, or whatever you have on your list, but you can at least do some planning and research. Find someone who's planning to climb Everest, purchase a round trip Seven Wonders of the World ticket, or email Mr Clapton's agent.

Towards the back of this book, under the section 'Putting It All Together', you'll find an example of what a typical Now List (planning) Day looks like (for me).

Rules of Now List Day

Like Boxing Day, Now List Day has rules to help you make it a success:

1. Now List Days/slots can be moved, but not cancelled
2. Only two things happen on a Now List day –
    a. you're either doing something on the list so that you can check it off, or
    b. you're planning/researching/booking items on your list for sometime in the future.

Ready to start turning those Now List ideas into memories? Let's do it:

STOP! ACTION POINT!

Book your Now List Days into your diary

Or Now List lunchtimes.
Breakfasts.
Evenings.
Whatever works for you.

The Trophy Board

Andy Warhol, so it's said, never opened any of his post. He merely collected it up, put it in a box, and when that box was full he sealed it and wrote the year on the top. When he died they found boxes and boxes of unopened post.

I've never taken the time to find out just how true this story is, but I do know that the first time I heard it, it had a profound effect on me and I wanted to do the same. However, being a somewhat deluded individual, I was fairly certain I could improve on the concept. Who, after all, would want to go through boxes of my unopened post?! Particularly when most of it would either be bills, red bills, final demands or letters from the utility companies informing me that I'd been cut off. I wanted my boxes to be full of interesting stuff.

And so I started to collect things. Ticket stubs mainly. Be they cinema or theatre tickets, raffle tickets, train tickets, plane tickets, pay-and-display parking tickets. But also postcards, greeting cards, thank you cards, business cards, labels, badges, old credit cards, menus, anything that was evidence of somewhere I'd been, something I'd done, or someone I'd seen or met.

I can't remember what I did with all this junk to start with but eventually (probably in an effort to retain some sort of control over the growing mountain of rubbish) I decided to get a really large cork notice board and pin this stuff to it. And there it hung in my living room - a huge messy board packed with memories. I loved it!

A few months later, on New Year's Day, I completed the last stage of my 'Andy Warhol' project by removing everything from the board, stuffing it in the largest envelope I could find, writing the year on the front in huge letters, and tossing it in the loft. A few days later I started the process again, pinning items to the board as I accumulated them.

Now, many, many years later, I have approximately twenty huge envelopes in the loft, each one with a year written on the front, and each one packed with papery mementoes. Do I ever look in these envelopes. No. Will I? No. What's the point then?

The point isn't the envelopes. The point is the board. On the following page I present to the reader exhibit A:

EXHIBIT A: MY TROPHY BOARD

That's 2010's board just before it was taken off the wall and all the items were tucked away in an envelope ready for the board to be repopulated throughout 2011. If you'd like to check my progress, visit the website at howtodoeverythingandbehappy.com.

Some might say this is clutter. I've heard self-help gurus tell people that this sort of stuff has no place in your life. But to me the board is my 'Trophy Cabinet'. It's a visual reminder of all the things I've done this year, and the space between the items is an opportunity to be filled with something else. When visitors come round they stand and admire the board. It's a conversation piece. Sometimes people ask me to explain an item. Nobody ever tells me it's a bad idea.

And when I'm tired, or feeling low, or I'm feeling a little like a hamster on a wheel, and that nothing I do ever amounts to anything, I look at the board and I realise that it's not true. Twenty fat envelopes in my loft say otherwise.

STOP! ACTION POINT!

How to Create a Trophy Board

Take a big cork board. Find somewhere to hang it. Then start pinning tickets, photos, postcards… anything that'll remind you of moments that you've enjoyed during the year.

What you put on the board doesn't have to relate to your Now List. The idea here is to create a visual reminder of how fun your life is. Don't be put off by its initial emptiness, it'll fill up faster than you think – see the emptiness as an opportunity waiting to happen.

At the end of the year (or when the board's full - whatever works for you), take the items off, and if you want to, bag them up, label the bag, throw it in the loft. When your ceiling gives way under the weight and you're showered in plaster and papery items you'll smile knowing how fulfilling your life has been.

Taking the trophy board one step further

I love the messiness of the board. I love its randomness. I love how friends stand in front of it and see if they can find anything new. But I understand that there are those amongst you (with Virgo tendencies) who wouldn't be able to see past the scraps of paper. For you it would always be clutter – a mess – hanging on the wall.

So consider this. It doesn't have to be a board. Here are some other ideas I've experimented with.

Photos

When I was a kid cameras needed to be loaded with film. You could only take 36 pictures before the film was full and had to be developed – which cost money. Needless to say, as every single photo was being paid for out of my paper round money I thought very carefully about every image I took.

These days, however, photography is cheap. It's rare for me to go anywhere without a digital camera of some description. If I haven't got my trusty little compact Canon, my phone can do a fairly decent job at snapping the odd memory.

And I'm not the only one. My dear old Dad is the only member of my family who isn't packing a camera somewhere about his person whenever the family get together. Even my nephew and niece (who are six) have digital cameras.

Now more than ever aspects of my life are photographed from every angle several times a week, and not just by me, but also by friends and family.

So here's what I did recently. I spent a pleasant afternoon looking through pictures and every time I found one that made me smile I copied it into a different folder. Then I found one of those online photo printing companies (photobox.co.uk is pretty amazing), uploaded the photos to them, and I had them produce 6x4 prints. It cost me next to nothing – literally only pence per print - to have about fifty images printed on glossy photographic paper and mailed to me. The quality was outstanding, far better than I could have ever achieved myself.

My absolute favourites got pinned to the fridge, or on the wall in my office. The remainder I filed. Periodically I rearrange the photos, or replace them with fresh ones. At some point I'll print up some new ones.

For the clutter-phobic amongst you, you could consider investing in a digital photo frame. They're like laptop monitors without the keyboard attached. You simply insert a memory card into the back and the frame should cycle through your images like a screensaver on your computer.

At the time of writing these things vary in price and quality and I've discovered – to my detriment – that there isn't necessary a correlation between the two. However, if you manage to get a good one they're worth their weight in gold.

My advice is to avoid photo frames with built in speakers or rubbish that you don't need. You want the best screen quality you can get, at the cheapest price. Everything else is a bonus.

Jars

Not all mementoes can be pinned to a notice board, fridge or wall. Every now and then you'll pick up something altogether more three dimensional. Maybe a pebble from the beach. A pocket full of Lipa (Croatian pennies). A finger puppet your niece made for you. A cork from a bottle of champagne. The security pass from the time you did a telly interview.

Don't throw these items into a drawer. Instead get yourself an old fashioned glass sweet jar and start filling it with this kind of stuff.

Not blowing your skirt up? Ok. I can respect that. Try this for size:

Printer's Tray

Back in the old days (I'm talking really old - older than me - long before computers, one might even say 'back in ancient times'), newspapers were printed by taking small blocks of metal, each of which had a letter embossed in the bottom, and laying these blocks side by side in a tray to form words and sentences. The blocks were wedged together, inked, and the paper quite literally 'stamped'.

As you can imagine, setting type must have been a time consuming business. So to speed things up it was essential that these little metal blocks were organised. And so they were. They were kept in specially made drawers – trays – which themselves were divided into sections.

What happened to these trays once the world went computerised? Well, most were cast to one side. Some were probably chopped up to make firewood. Others are probably on a landfill site somewhere. A few, however, ended up being sold at boot fairs, and antique markets, and on eBay. I've just done a search and found 193 on sale, for about a tenner each.

And why should you care?

Printer's trays are absolutely perfect for all those little nick knacks I mentioned above. Get yourself a tray, clean it up with wire wool, then screw it to the wall, and pretty soon you'll have something like the one on the following page.

Unlike the photos and the Year Board, the items in the printer's tray tend to stay in the same place year after year with only the occasional purge or addition. But that's just me. I can't even remember the significance of some of the items in the tray, but in a way I kinda like that. Like there's a memory there that's locked away and could only be retrieved by a particularly gifted hypnotist or psychic.

EXHIBIT B: MY PRINTER'S TRAY

Feeling Happier Yet?

So how are you? How are you feeling? How's your Now List looking? Got anything planned? Checked any items off yet? And whilst I'm firing off questions, when was your last Boxing Day? Really? Maybe you should have another one soon, eh?

If this all feels like "frosting", as Americans would call it - if it feels a little like we're filling our days with sugary treats but no real substance, or covering over our fundamentally sad existence with a layer of sickly sweet icing - then I respectfully ask you to give me one last chance. Because in the next section we're going to break through the icing and the marzipan, and move into the cake.

We're going to tackle the big stuff.

We're going to find out what it is that you actually want.

Pointing Your Life in a Better Direction

"To be truly radical is to make hope possible rather than despair convincing."
Raymond Williams. Welsh Novelist & Critic 1921-1988

What Do You Want?

What is it that you want? Right now?

Maybe you want a nice cup of tea, the people next door to turn down their music, and an end to war, poverty and Maria Carey cover versions? These are all good.

But what about your life?

What would make it better?

What would make you happier?

What do you want?

Most people I encounter haven't actually got a clue what they really want. They might wake up in the morning and *want* to go back to bed. They might flick through a magazine and *want* those shoes. They might even *want* the person, in the magazine, wearing those shoes. But these desires come and go. Few of them seem to stick around and become important - which is odd because when you're growing up, figuring out *what you want* is very important and actively encouraged.

"What do you want for Christmas?"

"What do you want to do today?"

"What do you want to be when you grow up?"

A huge part of being a kid is spent working out what we want, and then writing it down or telling someone about it. And yet, as we get older, and we're finally in a position to do something about the bigger 'wants' of our childhood, we seem to give the question less and less thought. As if the day-to-day grind of making ends meet is more than enough to occupy every waking minute.

And that's a mistake.

Knowing exactly what you want is hugely important. Merely *knowing* has the power to change *everything*.

Not convinced? Then allow me to introduce you to the incredible, completely automated wish-fulfilment machine you have inside your head.

The Power of Focus

Brains are amazing. Especially yours. Even mine has its moments. And one of the most fascinating mechanisms of the human brain is how it deals with 'focus'.

Have you ever noticed how when you buy a new car, or even when you've merely decided what type of car it is you want to buy, you start seeing that same car everywhere?!

Or the kettle packs up, the DVD stops playing, and suddenly half a dozen other electrical items in the house decide to turn up their boots, like they're all suffering from some sort of appliance manic depression.

Or how you can sleep through a thunderstorm, the traffic noise, and the sounds of revellers returning from a night on the town, but if your newborn's breathing changes even slightly – *in the next room* - you're awake!

Or have you ever seen someone across a crowded room, started to walk towards them, and somehow walked into the table, the person, the immoveable object, that was directly in front of you but momentarily invisible?

Or have you ever fallen in love, fallen out of love, had a tiff, a blazing row, a passing thought about that girl you used to know – and the words of the next song on the radio seem to capture your feelings precisely?

That's the power of focus. Your brain is extremely good at noticing things, or disregarding things, depending on whatever it is you're currently focused on.

The Science of Focus

'Focus' happens because in order for our brains to cope with the extraordinary amount of information coming in through our five senses from the world around us, we're programmed to concentrate on what's 'important' and more or less ignore the rest.

Unconvinced? Excellent!

Pick a card from the six on the opposite page. Don't tell me which one it is, just pick one, and remember which card you've chosen.

No, don't pick the King of Spades, everyone picks that one! Pick a different card.

Ready?
Now turn the page.

And it's gone!

But curiously enough, so has the King of Spades, and yet there are still five cards left. How is that possible?

Before you start flipping backwards and forwards between pages to figure out how I did that (if you haven't figured it out already), have you got access to the internet? If so, log onto www.howtodoeverythingandbehappy.com/focus and watch the short Selective Attention video. When you're done, you can come back here and turn the page.

**WARNING: TURNING THE PAGE
BEFORE WATCHING THE VIDEO
WILL RENDER THE EXPERIMENT USELESS**

So, what's going on in your head that you can watch a short video of kids playing basketball and utterly fail to notice something so obvious? The answer, of course, is 'focus'. Your mind was concentrating on something else, just as in the card trick you were concentrating on the card you'd chosen, and its apparent disappearance, and failed entirely to notice that all the cards had changed. The other cards weren't 'important'.

You might be asking yourself how does the brain determine what's important? And the answer is: you tell it! In both of the experiments it was you who chose what to focus on.

And this mechanism isn't just taking place during card tricks and baseball games; this happens all day, every day. Your brain is continually filtering the information coming into it based on what you've decided is important.

Strange then that we quite often focus on entirely the wrong things, or nothing at all.

Focusing on the wrong things

It's a curious thing but in driving incidents where a motorist loses control of their vehicle (say, in icy conditions) it's surprising how often they manage to hit a solitary tree, lamp post, or other static object, when statistically they should have been far more likely to have come to a halt on the other side of the road, or in a field.

This is because in those crucial seconds when they're spinning out of control your average driver will concentrate on trying *not* to hit the tree or the lamp post. Put another way, their focus will be on the very thing they don't want to hit, and as a consequence - they hit it!

This might seem crackers to you – it did to me. Were I to skid off the road I too would be gripping the steering wheel, looking at that tree, and doing everything in my power to avoid it. But as any racing driver might tell you, what I should be looking at is *where I want to be.* i.e. the road.

This isn't just a top driving tip; this goes for life in general. What you should focus on is where you want to be.

It might sound obvious, it might even be what you *think* you're doing, but I'd wager that the majority of people go through life focusing on the very thing they don't want.

Have you ever started a sentence with the words "I don't want..." or "If only I wasn't..." or "There has to be something better than..."? If so, you are focusing on what you DON'T want, and consequently you're subconsciously steering your life in the wrong direction. It's how the brain works. It's almost as if the brain can't process 'the negative' element. 'Don't hit that tree' becomes 'hit that tree'.

Did I hear someone make a comment about manure? Not convinced, eh? Ok. Try this simple experiment. Ready?

DO NOT THINK ABOUT A BOX OF FROGS.

I'll bet my book royalties that by the time you made it to the end of the sentence there was a box of frogs sitting slap bang in the middle of your imagination.

It simply isn't possible to *not* focus on something. The very act of NOT thinking about something requires your brain to conjure up images of the thing you don't want to think about, so it can ignore it.

The only way to avoid focusing on the wrong thing is to switch your focus to something else. Which, it has to be said, is far easier said than done. Particularly if you've made focusing on the wrong things a habit.

Earlier this year I went away for a few days with a friend who really struggles to focus on the positive. One afternoon, as we sat outside a bar, drinking cold beers in the blazing heat, my friend - who had somehow failed to enjoy two days of glorious sunshine, fantastic food, and bustling streets - turned to me and said, "So, what would you say has been your biggest disappointment of this holiday?"

It wasn't a question I wanted to answer. Yes, there were things that I could have thought of – if I'd tried - but the question revolted me. I didn't want to start making a list of *disappointments*; for one thing, my travelling companion would have been at the top of the list! But more than that, it would have meant focusing on the wrong things. It would have been telling my brain to be on the lookout for 'disappointments', to expect a negative outcome - just as they had - and pretty soon I'd have been sitting there feeling just as miserable.

Your brain is amazing. It'll take you in whatever direction you tell it. And if, like my friend, you've got into the habit of telling it to fill your days with disappointment, failure, worry and sadness it'll definitely deliver. However, you can use that *same* mental process to turn your life around by focusing on an outcome you actually want – my wife used to say "Worry about things going well."

Continuously focus your brain on the outcome you want and you'll find yourself achieving goals, experiencing success and feeling happier.

Focusing on nothing

Allow me to tell you another tale.

It had been twenty years since we'd last seen each other.

A lot can happen in twenty days, even twenty minutes can be quite eventful, so it was probably unreasonable to expect to cover the events of twenty years in the time it took to drink a mug of hot chocolate. It was, however, just enough time to get the general gist, and the gist was this: in those twenty years things hadn't worked out so well for my friend. She was very, very unhappy.

Life hadn't been a disaster - not in the slightest - but it certainly wasn't where she hoped it would be. She had a part-time job she didn't really enjoy. She was married to a man she wasn't in love with. And they lived in a house that was far too small, in a rough little neighbourhood, miles from anyone.

I couldn't understand it. When we were at school this girl had everything going for her – she was smart, funny, gorgeous – somehow it just didn't make sense that her life wasn't more... well, more!

And so we met for coffee again. And again. And again. And each week she'd tell me how this year's holiday would once again be spent in a caravan in Bognor. Not that there's anything wrong with Bognor, but after fifteen years it was beginning to lose its sparkle.

Or how, just for once, it would be nice to watch TV without having to move the computer desk first.

Or how every time she climbed into a bubble bath for a long soak one of the kids, even her husband, always needed to use the toilet. If only they had a downstairs loo...

The list went on.

And on.

After the third week my sympathy was beginning to wane. It wasn't that my friend was complaining about nothing – her gripes were, in many ways, justified. And if her situation had been brought about by a spell of rotten luck - something outside of her control - I'd have gushed sympathy till it came out of my ears, but from what I could see every single unsatisfactory element of her life had been the consequence of a decision that she had, at some point, been involved in.

For instance, fifteen years of Bognor Holidays was something she'd elected to do – her and her husband. True, her husband is a man who's a little stuck in his ways. True, their budget was quite limited. But it was hard to believe that a caravan in Bognor was the *only* family holiday option available, for fifteen years running.

Likewise the tiny house. At some point a decision had been made to buy that house, in that area. Again, finances had been an issue, *but there would have been options*. Surely? But from what I could discern, my friend had actually let her husband find and pick the house.

And let's talk about him - the husband. You might be wondering if she'd married a man who *changed*, or turned out to have a wicked streak. That can happen. Happens all the time. But from what I could tell she never really liked him. Ever. But she'd married him anyway. In fact, it would be more accurate to say he'd married her, and she'd merely turned up at the church at the allotted time.

It was thoughts like these that would float around my head as I sipped my hot chocolate and listened to another episode of 'woe is me'. And as our coffee meet-ups appeared to be getting longer and longer, I had more and more time to dwell on my friend's predicament. Until one day she said:

"I like our coffee meet ups. I get so bored during the day."

"Bored?" I replied.

"God, yes." I bit my lip. Boredom is a concept I have strong feelings about.

"So, what does your typical day involve?" I asked.

"Well, obviously I have to get the kids up," she said.

"Of course," I said.

"And make their sandwiches."

"Very important."

"And make sure they have everything they need – PE kits – books..."

"Sure," I said.

"Then I have to take them to school."

"Right."

"Then I might have to take them to their afterschool clubs.."

"Uh huh."

"Help them with their homework."

"Mmm."

"Then I cook dinner, tidy up, get things ready for the morning, then we're into our bedtime routine -"

"Ok, ok – what about whilst they're at school?"

"Well, Tuesday and Thursday I work in the shop…"

"Yes."

"Wednesday I see you."

"For an hour."

"Or two," she said with a smile.

"Ok. And the rest of the time?" She thought for a moment. Thought really hard. I was expecting her to tell me how much work it was to keep the house tidy, or maybe she went shopping, or visited her mother -

"Well, I guess I might watch a bit of telly. Maybe read a magazine?" And there it was. That told me everything I needed to know. The real answer to what my friend did with her time, aside from all the things she *had* to do, in the morning, and the evenings, was *precisely nothing.*

In fact 'precisely nothing' was the effort she'd put in to taking charge of her life from the very moment she left school. Her holidays, her house, even her husband was a direct result of absolutely zero effort on her part.

Put like that, her life didn't seem so bad – in fact, her life was an absolutely fabulous return on her zero investment.

It's easy for me to sound righteous here, but in fact there are many, many examples I could use from my own life where, due to a total lack of effort, *lack of focus*, on my part, I ended up with a situation that was less than satisfactory. I call it Living by Default.

Living by Default appears to happen whenever we assume that things will work out ok because *they should*, and/or we've expended very little effort on deciding what it is in life we actually want.

For instance, when I was a much younger man I naturally assumed that I would meet someone, fall in love, get married and have kids. I wasn't particularly fussy about who that someone might be, how or when this great romance was going to happen, or anything about the kids other than there would probably be some. I was just happy to wait and let it happen. That was, after all, how life was supposed to work.

It was only when I got to 35 and noticed that people had stopped describing me as an "eligible bachelor" and started instead to question my sexuality that I realised that there was quite a strong chance that the woman of my dreams was not going to knock on the door and invite herself into my life. Believe me when I tell you this was a shock. Due to my complete and total lack of focus on the relationship front, Life had delivered to me my default setting – i.e. no one.

My friend Wendy says that "A life lived in fear is a life half lived." I'd like to suggest that Living by Default has the potential to be worse. You only have one life. And if you choose to let it take you where it wants, like a leaf floating in a stream with dreams of someday reaching the ocean, that's your decision to make – just don't complain to me if you find yourself trapped on the rocks, or snagged by overhanging branches.

If, on the other hand, you'd rather not leave your happiness to chance, well that's an altogether more exciting attitude and something I'd very much like to be a part of.

What are you waiting for? Let's get started.

And where do we start?

By figuring out what it is you actually want.

Making a Wish List

Imagine that, in a moment of madness, you've decided to start redecorating. And I don't mean just slapping a fresh coat of paint on the walls – I mean major changes to your living space, the sort that involve a lump hammer being taken to that annoying dividing wall – and, in the process of undermining the structural integrity of your home, you discover an ancient-looking oil lamp within the wall cavity. You take off your rubber goggles, pick up the lamp, give it a rub and hey presto - an eight foot genie is standing amongst the plaster and broken tiles.

"Master," he says, "I have the power to grant thee three wishes." Three wishes? you think. That's handy.

So what would they be?

Now, don't just sit there staring into space whilst you ponder that. *This is important* and requires a little more than reeling off the first three things that come to mind. The genie isn't going anywhere – you have some time, so let's do this properly.

Write down everything

Grab a pen and a piece of paper and just start writing things down. Go ahead - you can do this now whilst you read this book. If you haven't got a pen or paper to hand (and it's too much effort to reach for the drawer that you keep your collection of cheap biros in) then create a "note" on your mobile phone, or whatever gadget you have to hand. If you happen to be sitting in a café, squirt some ketchup on a napkin and use a breadstick like a quill pen. Whatever it takes. But you need to be able to jot down some thoughts, whatever comes into that mind of yours when faced with the question on the following page:

Don't overthink it – write down everything. And I mean *everything*. Because it turns out that whilst genies enforce a three wish limit, there's nothing to stop you coming back for a second or third round of wishes. It's a bandwidth issue. Not storage. You can, in fact, have as many wishes as you like, limited only by the bounds of your own lifetime. So go wild.

There are two important things you need to bear in mind.

IMPORTANT THING NUMBER 1:
YOU'LL BE DOING A LOT OF THE WORK
(OR, AT THE VERY LEAST, ORGANISING IT).

(Sorry about that. Previous stories about genies granting wishes with little or no effort on the part of the wisher were a slight exaggeration.)

IMPORTANT THING NUMBER 2:
ALL WISHES HAVE TO BE WITHIN
THE BOUNDS OF POSSIBILITY
AND PHYSICS.

So, for instance, whilst '*Become invisible so I can sneak into Wembley Football Stadium*' might seem like a fantastic wish, one that would significantly add to your quality of life, unless you're willing to put in a significant amount of effort into discovering how to bend light around yourself at will, it might be a whole lot quicker and easier to change your wish to "*get a season ticket to Wembley*".

You started writing yet? Come on. You can write and read. How about you write down three things before you continue?

Chunk down

It's often useful to break your wishes into smaller sub-wishes, or to create a list of related wishes.

For instance, you might write:
Learn to play an instrument.
Then follow it up with:
Learn to play the guitar.
Then follow it up with:
Buy a guitar!
Then follow it up with:
Play in a band
Then follow it up with:
Write a hit single and tour the world.
..and these things are all great. Let's try not to get stuck on one train of thought though. Now that we've covered your musical ambition, let's move onto something else. What else would you like?
What do you want?

Sell yourself short. Or long

Some people, when faced with a task like this, engage in some 'inner censorship'. They go to write down what they want – and then they stop themselves. And ninety nine times out of a hundred it's because of fear.

Fear of ridicule from others.
Fear that their wishes might be impossible.
Fear of setting themselves up for some future failure.

Fear of acknowledging some inner voice that they've spent a lifetime ignoring.

Let me try and relieve you of that fear.

This is *just a list.* That's all. Just a piece of paper with thoughts on it. We're just writing things down. And – unless you have a burning desire to do otherwise – this is your Wish List *and should remain private*!

So, this being the case, it's fine to think big.

Want to walk on the moon? Write that down. Become President? Of the world? Write that down. Show Mariah Carey how to cover a record without butchering it? Definitely write that down.

It's also fine to think small.

So you really want those shoes? Fine! Shoes are important. Write that down! You want time to watch Eastenders each evening? I can't think of anything worse, but it's not *my* list - write it down. You want to read more often, get out in the garden once a week, work your way through all those Jamie Oliver cookbooks – then for heaven's sake, *write those things down.*

Stay in the positive

It's a funny thing about working out what we want. It's often easier to think about what we *don't* want.

People will say things like:

"I don't want to work another day in this crappy dead end job!"

Or: "I don't want to come home to a pile of problems and things that need sorting out!"

Or: "If I hear Mariah Carey on the radio one more time I am going to scream!"

But none of these things are "*what you want*" – instead, as we discussed earlier in the chapter, they're focusing your mind on the very opposite.

But, you might be thinking, isn't figuring out what you DON'T want a good place to start?

For instance, if your crappy dead end job is getting you down then surely a better job – one where you're valued and appreciated, and there are prospects – would be something you *want*, right?

If you don't want to come home to a pile of problems, isn't it only reasonable to assume that you'd prefer to come home to... something else? Maybe your spouse and your kids lined up, ready to greet you?

If the radio's playlist is getting you down then surely what you want is... better tunes on the radio? A different radio station? A CD player? An iPod?

Not necessarily.

People fall into two distinct groups. Those that 'run away from' things, and those that 'run towards' things.

Most people, myself included, are in the first group. This isn't necessarily a bad thing. By and large, a 'running away from' strategy will work, and keep you safe, *in the short term*. If, for instance, you're out foraging for food and you happen to see a sabre tooth tiger in the undergrowth, a 'running away from' strategy is a very good thing.

It's not so great when it comes to figuring out what you want from life though. And (as in the examples above) merely working out the 'wants' from the 'don't wants' is still nothing more than a 'running away from' strategy in disguise.

Using a 'running away from' strategy to chart the course of your life is a little like embarking on a journey to some far flung destination merely by trying to get as far away from your current location as possible, and without knowing where you want to get to. It might work - maybe - but it's extremely unlikely. To stand any real chance of ending up in the right place you need to know exactly where you want to be and, if possible, a general direction.

Keep your wishes in the positive. If it helps, start each sentence with the words "I want" and beware of any sentences that contain negative words such as "stop", "not", or "end".

For instance, you might think you want to *quit* smoking. And there are many, many people in this world who have done exactly that. They quit smoking, and they're still *quitting*. They've been counting the minutes, days, sometimes years, since their last cigarette. It's as if at any moment they might crack under the pressure of not smoking, grab the nearest packet of Marlboros, light one up, and cough a huge sigh of relief.

I'd like to suggest that maybe what you *really* want is to 'be a non-smoker'. Non-smokers don't live their lives in the shadow of the last cigarette, they just live. Usually for longer. They don't even think of themselves as *non*-smokers, in the same way that I don't think of myself as a *non*-female. Non-smokers are just... we're ... well, we're people who breath clean, regular air rather than anything else. There. Clean air breathers. That's what's we are.

Have a quick look at what you've written so far. If you've got any negative wishes on your list, consider weeding them out and then asking yourself what it is that you *really* want.

Engage your inner lawyer

Genies can be sneaky. If there's an easier way of granting your wish without actually achieving what you *really* meant that's exactly what will happen.

Let me give you an example.

You might say that you want to quit your boring office job.

No - you don't.

For one thing, that's a horrible negative wish, but much more seriously, for the Genie to grant that wish all he or she needs to do is arrange for you to be fired, or made redundant, leaving you without the boring office job and any form of income.

"Ok," you might say, "in that case, I want a better job."

Better? Better how? What if the Genie arranged for you to receive a promotion; more money, more responsibility, more hours...

"No, no, no," you say, "I want to work somewhere else, for more money, less hours, and within an hour of my home."

Excellent. In that case I have a vacancy that might interest you. You would be our Senior Clothing Research Technician with special responsibility for Mono-Chrome Fastening Devices for a small but select group of our customers. We need you to find and separate all the left-handed black and white buttons from this big pile in the corner.

To which you'd reply: "I want to *enjoy* working somewhere else for more money, less hours, and within an hour of my home."

Good for you. Now you're getting somewhere.

And you want that because?

So how many items have you got on your list so far?

Here's a little exercise for you. Run down the list and in your head ask yourself: "Why do I want this?"

Take Beth, for instance. At the top of her wish list she's written: "I want to date George Clooney."

And why do you want that, Beth?

Beth thinks long and hard about this (after I've dismissed her rather glib answer that George is 'fit' and what woman wouldn't want to be dating him!)

"Because I want a fit boyfriend," says Beth. And just like that we've uncovered an underlying wish. She wants a boyfriend. A fit one. Let's see if we can go deeper still. Why do you want a boyfriend? What's the wish beneath this one?

"Because I don't want to be alone."

That's a *'running away from'* strategy

"Because I want to share my life with someone nice."

Much better. And you want that because?

"That would make me happy."

All your wishes should eventually get back to this point. If they don't then I'd argue that they have no place on your Wish List. But think carefully before assuming that your desire for happiness is the layer beneath whatever wishes you have on your list – most wishes have several layers. This exercise can, when done carefully, uncover some very interesting, very personal desires that shed light on what it *really* is that would make you happy.

And that is, after all, the point of this book.

STOP! ACTION POINT!

Consider creating a wish list

Ask yourself the question: "What do you want?"

Keep in mind these important points:
1. You can have as many wishes as you want
2. Keep your wishes within the bounds of possibility and the laws of physics
3. Break your wishes into smaller and/or subsequent wishes
4. Think about all the different aspects of your life – don't get hung up on one thing
5. Feel free to think as big as you like
6. Or small. Be honest with yourself
7. Make all wishes positive – avoid 'running away from' strategies
8. Be absolutely clear on what you want. Leave the Genie no room to wiggle out. Engage your inner lawyer.
9. Think about the wish beneath your wish – the layer below. Is there something more fundamental that should be on your list instead of, or as well as, the top layer?

What Do You Want - Right Now?

Let's take a break from your Wish List for a moment, and
think instead about what you want, *right this second.*

Go ahead, take a moment to think about what you want
right now. It could be that you want me to stop waffling on
about 'lists' and get on with the part where I tell you how to
get your wishes granted. It could be that you want someone to
bring you a toasted cheese sandwich and a cup of tea. Or it
could be that you simply want the sun to come out again –
dammit!

Knowing what you want in any given moment is, I've
discovered, a hugely underrated skill.

Have you ever had days when you start with a pretty clear
idea of what the next few hours have in store for you, only to
discover that the universe has other plans? The phone starts to
ring, your email inbox starts to fill up, now there's someone at
the door – everybody either wants you to do something, wants
to tell you something, wants your opinion on something,
wants to sell you something.

If, like me, you live and die by your to-do list you find
yourself adding more items than you're checking off. By mid-
afternoon you've done nothing but answer the phone and talk
to people. Your desk is a sea of post-it notes. You can no
longer see the top of your inbox. You're drowning.

Or perhaps you're having a day that's the total opposite.
The phone isn't ringing. There aren't any emails. There are
only two items on your to-do list. Neither of them are very
inspiring. You feel like your brain's made of porridge.

Both these situations can be fixed by asking yourself one simple question:

WHAT DO YOU WANT?
RIGHT NOW?

Your initial answer, of course, will probably be something like "I want it to stop" - either the chaos, or the boredom - but you need to dig a little deeper than that. Try and get to the bottom of what would make a huge difference to you, either at that moment, or in the near future.

For instance, on your chaotic day simply knowing what it is you most want allows you to prioritise all the stuff coming 'in'. If the stuff relates to whatever it is you want, prioritise it; if it doesn't, chuck it on the backburner. Pretty soon you're like a ninja: sword-wielding bad guys might be coming at you from every angle, but you're only paying attention to those that present you with an opportunity.

On those 'boring' days, however, you can take your thinking about what you want to a whole new level. You can write things down. You can make lists. You can toss ideas about. You're like a ninja in training – mentally preparing yourself. It'll only be a matter of time before you realise one of the ideas you're toying with is something you can do, right now, on this boring day.

STOP! ACTION POINT!

What do you want? Right now?

Next time you find yourself drowning in work, or plodding along with no real purpose, stop, and ask yourself what it is that you want, right now.

How you remember to do this is up to you. Above my desk I have a small piece of paper with the words "what do you want?" typed out in colourful letters.

The Power of Three

Back to your Wish List. Hopefully what you have in front of you is a page or two (maybe more) full of 'wishes'.

Now the work really begins.

Pick three of your wishes

Take a fresh sheet of paper (open a new document, create a new note - whatever) and, referring back to your wish list, pick out the three "wishes" - just three - that you would like to achieve first. We'll come back to the others later, I promise, but for now pick the three things from your list that you want most in life.

So, for instance - getting back to your musical ambitions - whilst all the things you wrote down were great, (the world tour sounds absolutely fab - please feel free to invite me to the after show party) 'learn to play the guitar' is an obvious first step on your road to fame and fortune, and would therefore make a good first *wish*.

Try and make sure that the items you pick are achievable in the next year or two. Whilst I don't have a problem with long term wishes they have a nasty habit of staying long term. So if your wish is 'world domination' - and you realise that this might take four or five years to achieve - create a smaller wish first: 'purchase island in the South Pacific and build evil mastermind lair' or 'create robot army' springs to mind.

Pick three different areas of your life

It's up to you, but I like to pick three wishes that reflect three very different areas of my life. Say, my work life, my personal life, and... something else.

Why only three?

You're probably wondering why I've limited you to three wishes. Why spend all that time creating a 30 page wish list if at the end of the day you're only going to work on three of them at once? Why not work on them all?!

The sad fact is there is only one of you. Only one person to get the work done. To have the absolute best chance of success, when it comes to turning your wishes into reality you need to limit how many you work on simultaneously.

Like everything in this book, I learnt this lesson by bitter experience. Not so long ago my 'daily' to-do list ran to *sixteen pages of A4*. As you might expect of a man who's quite keen on organisation and planning, the list was basically every single thing I had to do for every project and goal I wanted to achieve. As a result my days quite often felt like I was nudging several hundred dominos forward a centimetre at a time, and when I had nudged forward the last domino I would collapse into bed, weary and dejected, only to start again the following day.

Nothing in my life seemed to move forward very fast.

Then I listened to "Work Less, Make More[19]", by Jennifer White, and was intrigued by a principle called "the power of three": Concentrate on only three things at once, says Jennifer. Just three. Within each project focus only on the three tasks that will help you complete the project. If these tasks can be broken down further – into sub-steps – concentrate on only three of those steps. Everything else goes on the backburner.

"The power of three," says Jennifer, "will set you free."

You can use 'the power of three' in almost everything, and it's especially powerful if you're the kind of person who finds it easy to start something, but difficult to finish. Implement this principle and you simply won't be able to start something new until at least one of your existing three 'projects' is complete.

For instance, if you've bought a wreck of a house and you plan to renovate the whole thing, the power of three would dictate that you pick only three rooms to start with – maybe the kitchen, the bathroom and a bedroom. Within those three rooms you'll pick a maximum of three tasks to start and complete; so within the bathroom you might decide to rip out the existing suite, chip off the old tiles and replace the windows – but you won't start pulling up the floorboards and messing with the pipes until one of the other items is complete.

My house decorating analogy might not work in reality – DIY is not my strong suit. However, I implemented the power of three into my mammoth to-do list and suddenly my life

---

[19] 'Work Less, Make More' by Jennifer White. Publisher: John Wiley & Sons (4 Nov 1999). ISBN-13: 978-0471354857

started moving forwards. As of today the to-do list is only 6 pages long (I just checked).

But I digress. Back to wishes… time for you to do some work.

STOP! ACTION POINT!

Pick three wishes from your Wish List

➢ Pick the three that are the most important to you
➢ *Consider* picking three wishes from different 'areas' of your life

Using the Power of Focus

Remember we talked about your brain's extraordinary ability to focus? Of course you do. It was only a few pages ago. And this being the case – being the wonderfully astute person that you are – you're probably wondering if we can use this power of focus to make all those things on your Wish List come true.

The answer is yes – yes we can.

There are numerous techniques I use, the most powerful of which is to take your three wishes and turn them into 'goals'. We'll look at this in the next section; for now, however, I want to reiterate that *simply knowing* what it is that you want has already started to re-programme your subconscious. You'll be surprised at how this affects what you notice, or don't notice, over the next few days.

But just to be sure, here are three easy suggestions to help get those wishes into your head and reinforce your power of focus.

Review your three wishes every day

How you do this is up to you, but see if you can create a habit whereby you remind yourself of your top three wishes. Good times to do this might be…

- As you brush your teeth (shower, blow dry your hair…)
- As you drive to work (walk to the station, drive the kids to school…)
- As you walk up the stairs (a different wish for each flight of steps, maybe)

The Wish Board

Remember the Trophy Board we created in the Now List section? The board covered with ticket stubs, photos, and all manner of Now List memorabilia? It's worth creating a second board stuffed with imagery of what you'd like in your life. For many years my wife and I had a board like this in our kitchen.

A Wish Board like this works in two ways – not only is the board itself a visual reminder of your wishes, but the act of keeping an eye out for appropriate images as you leaf through magazines is in itself an exercise in programming your subconscious.

Another way to find Wish Board imagery is to use your computer. Bring up Google and perform an image search.

And if you're computer literate and spend your day staring at a screen, as I do, you might as well do this.

The Wish Screensaver

Your computer has a screensaver. We can use that. Having gone to the effort of finding different images[20] related to your wishes - maybe several images per wish - save those images into a folder and use the slideshow screensaver (almost every computer has one) to display these pictures whenever the computer's idle.

---

[20] To save a picture from a webpage, right click the image – you'll usually be offered the option to save the image on your computer.

STOP! ACTION POINT!

Harness your power of focus!

Knowing what you want momentarily points your subconscious in the right direction. Reminding yourself creates more of those moments.

➢ Find time, once a day, to run through your three wishes in your head
➢ Consider creating a Wish Board
➢ Create a Wish Screensaver

Potential Wish List Problems

Right now, I estimate there's an 80% chance that you'll be basking in the clarity of having worked out exactly what it is that you want out of life. Over the coming days your family and friends will pick up magazines only to notice that pages or parts of them appear to be missing where someone has hacked out an inspirational image. People will catch you sitting in front of your computer watching the screensaver, or talking to yourself in front of the bathroom mirror. And you'll start to notice 'stuff'.

For instance, maybe you've already noticed that there's a car, pretty much identical to the one you've always wanted, sitting in the showroom of that second hand car dealership just down the road. Or the local college is running an evening class in South American basket weaving, a skill you've always wanted to develop – what were the chances? Or last night you happened to overhear a guy in the pub telling someone how he's planning on starting a petition to ask Mariah Carey to cease from making any more cover versions. This is the power of focus at work. Your subconscious is busy identifying things that you've deemed important to you, and putting them on the radar of your mind, in case you want to do something about it.

Now, whilst 80% is a fairly good percentage, I can't really continue without trying to address the 20% of people who are sitting there with a bewildered, grumpy or downright frustrated expression on their face. If you're one of them bear with me for a page or two whilst we go over some common wish list problems.

I'm confused! What's the difference between my wish list and my Now List?

You might find that having diligently written your Now List in the previous section, you now want to write exactly the same things on your wish list. Is that ok?

Possibly.

Your Now List is the answer to this question:

WHAT WOULD I LIKE TO EXPERIENCE BEFORE I DIE?

Your Wish List is the answer to this question:

WHAT DO I WANT {IN MY LIFE} OR {MY LIFE TO BE}?

Now it may be that, when faced with either question, you immediately think "climb Mount Kilimanjaro". And that's just fine. Clearly climbing this mountain is an experience - therefore making your Now List - and you obviously feel so strongly about it that when faced with a genie this would be your first wish - thereby making your wish list.

In practice, however, it doesn't *really* matter. If, by putting an item on your Now List and/or your wish list, it ends up being something that you do, and that makes you happy – then good for you. My work here is done.

I've got more to say on this subject, but I'd like to come back to it at the end of the next section if that's ok with you.

It's all me, me, me, me, me

It's no fun growing up with brothers and sisters. Life is a constant battle for supremacy. And whilst being the eldest, or the tallest, or the strongest, should give you the competitive edge amongst your siblings, there's always a parent hovering in the background who's just one squabble away from wading in and levelling the playing field with a clip round the ear and comments such as:

"Wait your turn," or

"Be nice to your sister," or

"How many times have I told you to share?!"

You can appeal, of course – I often did – but this was usually met with:

"Peter - not everything's about you," or

"If you can't play nicely then I'll take it away," or

"I want, I want, I want – that's all I ever hear!"

It seems that no sooner have we been encouraged to 'think for ourselves' and 'decide what we want in life' than someone, maybe the same someone, tell us that we're being self centred or selfish. 'Putting others first,' so they say, is the true path to enlightenment.

Now I'm not going to tell you that our parents were wrong - not entirely - but a few of us (and I include myself in this) had this concept of putting others first beaten into us so effectively that we've all but lost the ability to consider our own needs at all. And if we take a moment to go against our programming we pay a penalty with feelings of guilt.

What our parents should have told us was this:

**TAKING INTO CONSIDERATION OUR OWN WANTS,
TO THE EXCLUSION OF EVERYONE ELSE,
IS WRONG.**

The middle line of that sentence is crucial! Without it, you're effectively telling yourself that everyone else is more important than you – and whilst there will be those of you who actually believe that, <u>it's simply not true</u>.

Here's another thing your parents should have told you:

**TAKING INTO CONSIDERATION EVERYONE ELSE,
TO THE EXCLUSION OF YOURSELF,
IS UTTERLY, UTTERLY WRONG.**

No good can come of thinking of others to the exclusion of yourself. You will end up standing in the Personal Growth aisle of your local bookshop, real or virtual, considering books on how to become happier.

Now, let me just say that these are incredibly hard concepts to grasp if you've spent a lifetime putting others first. Even if your logical brain says, "Oh yes, I see now – I need to strike a balance" - your inner child will continue to follow the rules your parents laid down in the hope that one day they'll magically work for you. They won't. Unfortunately, undoing this level of brainwashing takes more than a couple of pages in a book like this.

So here are a few things you could try.

Firstly, there's therapy. And I'm not kidding. It really is the only way to free yourself from this noble, but none the less destructive, behaviour. However, therapy is like embarking on a long personal journey through your own psyche for which you really need a qualified and experienced guide. Finding a therapist that works for you can be a challenge. This isn't a reason not to try therapy, it's merely a warning – try, if you can, to see a therapist who someone you trust can recommend.

Secondly, you could leave yourself notes around your house or office to remind you of the two facts above. Will it work? Maybe. It's a low tech solution that won't remedy the underlying problem, but sometimes a sticking plaster is all that's necessary to enable us to continue on in life.

Lastly, you could strike a compromise with yourself. Accept the fact that there are other people in your life and incorporate them into your Wish List. Grab a piece of paper and instead of starting your wishes with the words "I want", try starting a few with "we want" and see where that gets you.

For instance:

"We want to travel the world."

"My mother and I live in a wonderful house, near the sea."

"I am learning to play the guitar, with the support of ..."

Knowing what you really want is hard!

Lucy says: "I find it utterly laudable in intention that you're inviting people to identify what they truly want and take responsibility for getting it - but I am brought up short by the fact that you make no reference to how HARD it is to find out what we really truly want, as opposed to what we are culturally invited to find desirable."

You're right. It is hard to find out what you really truly want. Perhaps it even borders on the impossible. So my advice to you is to STOP trying to find out what you '*really, truly want*' and instead answer the infinitely simpler question:

"WHAT DO YOU WANT?"

Don't overthink it. Don't edit yourself. Don't dismiss the first thought that comes to mind. This is a book on becoming happy, not spiritually fulfilled. If you want to *eat chocolate every single day*, write that down. If you want to *lose weight from a lifetime of eating chocolate every day,* write that down. Just ask yourself the question – then write! If you haven't got an answer by the end of this paragraph chances are you're thinking way too deep! You'll find the very act of creating a Wish List sparks off new ideas – and who knows, eventually one of them might be the Holy Grail that you're looking for, the thing you *really truly want.*

In the meantime, shift your focus away from "how difficult it is" and get writing.

The 'Universe' and its wicked sense of humour
It's a funny thing about the focus mechanism in your head, but as well as bringing to your attention all those things you've deemed important, you may find you start to notice all the things that are the complete opposite of what you want.

For instance, let's say that your three wishes basically amount to the same thing: "spend more time with the family." You created yourself a nice screensaver featuring pictures of you and the kids, and the walls of your office are now plastered with family photos. No sooner have you done this than your boss walks in and offers you a raise. And a promotion. And a new car. And an expense account. And a bigger office. In Dubai. For six months.

Now clearly this job in Dubai runs counter to your wish. It is, none the less, a very exciting opportunity. You might even do a little detective work to see whether or not you can take your family with you – only to discover that you can't. Should you take the job?

This scenario may seem unlikely but it's happened to me enough times to realise that there's a mechanism at work here. It's almost as if the Universe, God, or a deity of your preference, picks up your Wish List and says, "So this is what you really want, is it? So you wouldn't be the slightest bit interested in…" and ka-zaam! The total opposite of what you want is laid out before you, for the taking.

In moments like this I treat it for what it is.

A choice.

This is an opportunity to examine your heart. To think carefully about whether or not the items on your Wish List are things that you *really* want, or things that you *should* want. In short, it's time to be honest with yourself.

Whether you take the job in Dubai (or whatever your equivalent would be) is, of course, entirely up to you. And in my experience, decisions like this usually require a great deal of soul searching, usually when there's very little time to do anything of the sort. Worse still, even once you've made the choice there's nothing to stop the Universe (God, etc) coming back and asking you again, and again, and again, each time raising the stakes. That just seems to be how it works. So it's important to keep in mind the original question:

What is it that you really, really, want?

How is any of this nonsense supposed to improve my life?!!?
Ok, enough talk about 'the Universe'. Let's roll up our prayer
mats, exchange our orange robes for civilian clothing, and
think seriously about getting a haircut and having a shave.
Some people just aren't in touch with their inner hippy.

Those same people will struggle with the whole concept
of Wish Lists. And though I've done my best to show you that
there are some very real, proven psychological mechanisms at
play that underpin what some describe as 'the law of
attraction', it still feels like hocus pocus to many.

These people don't want to leave anything to shadowy
parts of their psyche. Pointing their life in the right direction
isn't enough. They want a step-by-step guide telling them how
to get from A to B - how to get what they want. They need
control, dammit!

And I can understand that. Because I'm one of them. And
if you are too, then grab that Wish List, turn the page, and
let's talk about how to go about changing your life.

Making Life What You Want

"Tell me, what it is that you plan to do
with your one wild and precious life?"
Mary Oliver. American poet b.1935

Does This Sound Familiar?

6am. The alarm goes off.

Surely it can't be 6am already? Surely not!

You reach for your watch. It too says it's 6am. Amazing. What were the chances? Both your alarm clock and your watch are running several hours fast.

Your partner nudges you in the ribs.

"It's six o'clock," they mumble. It is? It really is? And that's not good news because you know from experience that they are never, ever wrong.

An hour or so later you're sitting in your car. The radio burbles in the background, but you're listening to the rhythmic sound of the windscreen wipers whilst you stare at the brake lights of the car in front. After a while those lights go out and the car moves forward a couple of feet. You move your foot from the brake, squeeze the accelerator, take up the slack, and then stop again.

It's at this point that a thought floats through your mind. A thought that you will have several more times before you get to work, and numerous times throughout the day. It's a thought that you have so often you barely even notice it any more: "There must be more to life than this."

You Can Change Your Life

Here's something that you might find hard to believe:

YOU CAN CHANGE YOUR LIFE.

Some caveats: "You can change your life" isn't quite the same as "You can have the life you want."

I'm not saying you *can't* have the life you want – I'm just saying that it usually takes many, *many* 'changes' to get from where you are to where you want to be.

But theoretically, whether you want to climb Mount Everest, be the president of America, or create a time machine, there are a finite number of steps between 'here' and 'there' - you simply need to figure out what they are.

Quite often it's not even necessary to know all the steps before you take them – you merely need to know what the *next* step should be.

For instance, want to climb Mount Everest? Maybe the next step is to find someone who's done it before.

Want to be the president of America? Maybe the next step is to become an American citizen.

Want to create a time machine? Maybe the next step is to understand Quantum Physics, or buy a Delorean. Maybe both.

This section of the book isn't about figuring out what those steps are. Sorry about that. Unless I write another book, that's down to you. This section is about something far more fundamental: *making sure those steps happen*. But first let's refresh our memories on what you actually want.

Turning Wishes into Goals

Grab your Wish List from the last section. In fact, don't even
bother with the whole list – the only thing we're interested in
(for now) are those top three wishes.

What we're going to do in this section is to take those
wishes, and turn them into *goals*.

A lot of my friends dislike the idea of setting themselves
personal goals, like it somehow takes the private part of their
life, the part that is supposed to be about relaxing and having
fun, and turns it into 'work'. Which, as we all know, is the
mortal enemy of fun and relaxation. There will be those of
you who are already resisting this part of the book. You'll be
telling yourselves that you've "tried setting goals before."
That "it didn't work", or it "could never work", or that you're
simply "too busy."

If this is you then you have my sympathy. I used to feel
the same way. I've sat in traffic on the M25, morning after
morning, listening to those Tony Robbins CDs and wondering
whether I'd enjoy them more if I wound down the window
and tossed them, Frisbee-like, over the edge of the bridge and
into the River Thames far below me.

If you're feeling the same way we need to strike some
sort of bargain. Stick with me for a few more pages. Chances
are you will have never set goals in quite this way before -
even if you've listened to Tony Robbins or countless other
gurus. And even if you have, 'setting goals' is only the first
step. Crucial, yes, but only in the sense that getting in your car
and knowing where you want to go is the crucial first step to
any car journey. Later in this section I'll introduce you to a

slew of tricks and tools that'll help you turn those goals into reality and prevent them from being nothing more than a pointless list of 'nice to haves', but first we need to talk about 'wording'.

The vital importance of 'wording'

So you have your top three wishes. Surely to make them goals we just declare them as such and hey presto! Job done!

Not so fast, buster.

To be goals, real goals, we need to infuse them with power. We need to give them the ability to inspire you, move you, prod you, poke you, *irritate you* – whatever it takes, in fact, until they're no longer goals, but Statements of Fact: descriptions of how your life has become.

And how do we achieve this magic?

With words.

Let me introduce you to my friend Anne. She's an odd person. She actually liked the idea of setting goals! There wasn't any arm twisting involved. No sooner was she introduced to the concept than she came up with this list:

1. Be nicer to the kids
2. Listen to more live music
3. Lose weight

These are, on the face of it, very worthy goals. Worthy. But not particularly *useful*. Let's make them better.

Step 1: Make your goals personal

Right now Anne's goals are a little anonymous. They read like slogans. And whilst creating posters that read BE NICE TO YOUR KIDS might work, it's a little extreme. Let's save the World War II style advertising campaign for when we're desperate. Instead, we can boost the effectiveness of the goals just by adding two simple words - "I will"

1. I will be nicer to the kids
2. I will listen to more live music
3. I will lose weight

Now when we read these goals out loud they're no longer meaningless slogans, or commands, they're _commitments._ By saying them, even in your head, you're making a promise.

Don't take my word for it. Try it out. What's the one thing in your life that you would really like to change but you know in your heart you probably never will? Quit smoking? Walk the dog each evening? Phone your mother once a week? Now, plug the words "I will" in front of whatever it is you've just thought of and say it out loud.

Do it now.

Ok, ok, you don't _have_ to say it out loud - just say it in your head, but put this book down for a second and do it.

Done it? Ok. But did you _notice how uncomfortable it makes you feel?_ Did you notice that little knot in the pit of your stomach, or the niggle at the back of your mind, or the voice in your head that's saying "yeah right"? That's the kick back. That's the part of you that's *resisting* the change. That's the little kid in you who used to lie on the floor screaming when he or she didn't get his own way. All we've done is add two words and suddenly there's a part of your psyche that wants you to quit right now! Believe it or not, that's progress!

I have a friend who says, "Behind every no entry sign there's a door." By placing those two words in front of your goals you've created a door.

Step 2: Bring your goals into the present
If you think your psyche had a problem with "I will" just wait
and see what kind of fuss it'll make if you replace "I will"
with "*I am*".

When we do this to Anne's goals they look like this:

1. I am nicer to the kids
2. I am listening to more live music
3. I am losing weight

Perhaps the first thing to notice here is that you can't just swap
"I will" for "I am"; other words have to change too, and that's
because we're changing whole sentences from ones that talk
about this dim and distant point in the future when we'll be
nice to kids, where we're surrounded by live music, and our
excess weight is a thing of the past, to sentences that describe
things that have happened or are happening now.

Suddenly our goal about being nice to the kids isn't an
aspiration any longer – it's a reality. It's happening in the here
and now. We're no longer dreaming about how our days will
be spent listening to live music, it's something that happens
regularly. And we're no longer looking forward to shedding
those pounds, we're... hang on a second. I still don't like that
last goal. "I am losing weight"? We can do better than that.

3. I have lost weight

Much better. Nobody wants to be losing weight. Losing
weight is a drag – we want that weight gone!

"But," Anne might say to me, "it isn't true."

"What's not true?" I would reply.

"The sentence – it doesn't make sense."

"How so?"

"I haven't lost weight! I'm not nice to the children! And I'm not listening to live music!!" And then she'd probably shake me by the shoulders and I'd be forced to slap her to calm her down[21].

Of course it's not true. Yet.

What we're doing here is using a principle taken from hypnosis. The subconscious is a highly suggestible portion of your psyche. And if it's told something often enough, and with enough sincerity, it will eventually believe it. (You may have heard it described as 'brainwashing'.) This in turn will have a knock-on effect on your behaviour and the choices you make.

Can you brainwash yourself? Yes, you can. By setting our goals in the present, as if they're already fact, we're programming our subconscious to align our reality with what we want.

Resistance is futile

Still struggling with this? Who's still feeling some pangs of resistance?

Let's talk about that feeling because that too is a brain function. Perhaps the true reason for your resistance to writing goals in this way, whether you've realised it or not, is because you *might actually get what you want*, and part of your psyche doesn't want that to happen.

---

[21] Relax - I wouldn't slap her. But I might be forced to stuff a cream cake in her mouth.

Another peculiar function that the large walnut-like sponge in your head performs is the job of maintaining the status quo and keeping you exactly where you are. It's a defence mechanism. A kind of inbuilt "If it ain't broke, why fix it?" process. Everybody, to a lesser or greater degree, has an in-built resistance to change.

My personal resistance to change is incredible. Just wearing something a little different will have that voice in my head screaming at me, telling me that I'm totally bonkers, that no good can ever come of this radical change of image. I've learnt to recognise this voice. I use it to determine whether or not an idea or a course of action might achieve something. If I feel the resistance I know that the idea is likely to lead to change in my life. If I feel nothing, then it'll probably have no effect at all. Perverse though it might seem, it's become part of my mental tool box for making decisions.

Feeling the resistance? Good. Then let's move on.

Step 3: Make your goals measureable

So let's take another look at those newly worded goals of my friend Anne:

1. I am nicer to the kids
2. I am listening to more live music
3. I have lost weight

Having reworded them you might think that we've significantly increased the odds of Anne achieving them, but you'd be wrong. Whilst the new goals might be enough to motivate my friend into a frenzy of kid pleasing, music listening and weight losing activity, *how will she know when a goal has been met?*

For instance, let's take the last goal - "I have lost weight". If this were my goal, could I meet this goal by simply skipping dinner tonight? Tomorrow morning I would doubtless be a few grams lighter! Goal achieved? "Of course not," I hear you say, "that's cheating." Is it?

Let's take goal number two: "I am listening to more live music". If this were *my* goal and I went to one more concert this month than last month, would that be enough to meet this goal? Given that last month I didn't listen to any live music surely I've only got to see one band and I'm home and dry.

Then again, two months ago I went away to Glastonbury (the music festival) and saw more than a dozen bands. I had such a great time it's the reason I set this goal in the first place – so given this, how many bands do I have to see, and how frequently, for this goal to be achieved?

I'm lying, of course. It's not my goal – it's Anne's. I never went to Glastonbury, and the idea of sleeping in a tent, in a cold muddy field, live music or not, is not my idea of a good time. That's why I'm creating the following goal:

**PETER'S NEW PRIMARY GOAL:
I HAVE NOT BEEN CAMPING,
AT ALL,
IN THE LAST YEAR
(31ST DECEMBER, THIS YEAR)**

I am reasonably confident that I'll achieve this, because I know exactly what it is I have to achieve (zero camping) and by when (end of this year). Does Anne know what she has to achieve, and by when? No.

Hang on, you might say - if Anne set the goal "I am listening to more live music" then she'd have a fair chance of knowing when the goal was achieved. Maybe all she really wants is to be able to recall the last time she saw some live music – and for it to be recent enough that not only can she remember what she wore, but she still owns the outfit.

Likewise with the weight loss goal – surely on the day that she finds her clothes are so baggy that they weigh more than she does, she can declare this goal met. So why complicate things?

But notice what we've done here. Without even meaning to, we've worked out what our success criteria is for those two goals – Anne's clothes won't fit any more, but they will be the same clothes she wore to see a band not so long ago. That success criteria should be written into the goal – without it we can never be sure if the goal is met.

To illustrate the point further let's have a look at Anne's first goal – "I am being nicer to the kids".

Goals like this are extremely difficult to quantify. How will Anne know if she's being nicer to the kids? Having come from a business background my initial reaction would be to look for some sort of data source. When it comes to live music and weight loss there's a set of scales in Anne's bathroom and her social calendar hangs on the kitchen wall, but I don't think she keeps a record of the times she's lost her temper with the kids. So unless she's the sort of person who writes that stuff in a journal ("Dear diary, once again I completely lost my rag after little Johnny fed the goldfish to the cat.") the only thing she's got to go on is *memory*.

What's your memory like? Personally I have a hard time remembering my name. Pinned to the wall by the front door is a list of things to check before I leave the house. Seriously. That's not a joke. My wife made it for me after the hundredth time that I came back to the house to collect my phone, or my wallet, or my iPod. And those were the times when I could actually get back in because I'd remembered my keys. But I digress. The point is, can anyone really remember every spat they've had with the kids? Really? What, every one?

This is why working out the success criteria for your goals, *as you set them*, is essential. It forces you to face issues like this long before they become issues. And in the case of this goal there are really only two ways to ensure that Anne can measure it when the time comes:

1. She keeps a log of all the times she loses her temper with the kids, or
2. She writes a better goal!!

I really don't recommend keeping a list of arguments. In a book that's all about becoming happier, counting the number of arguments you have with your kids (or spouse, or boss, or anyone) is, once again, focusing on what you *don't want* – the arguments, the spats, your short temper – as opposed to what you *do want* which is... what exactly? *What is it you want?* More quality time? More fun? More laughs? Is that a "yes" I hear? Then let's chuck out Anne's horrible negative goal. I've seen Anne with her kids and she's a great mum! That nasty goal made her sound like some wicked old crone and that's simply not true. All she wants is more quality time with her children, and who could blame her? - in which case, the goal should look more like this:

1. The kids and I are doing something fun, every week (31st December, This Year).

Now that's a goal I can get behind! It's positive, it's personal, it's written in the present tense, it's definitely measureable, and it has a deadline.

Deadlines. Let's talk about that.

Step 4: Add a deadline to your goals

So Anne's revamped goals now stand as follows:

1. The kids and I are doing something fun, every week (31st December, this year)
2. I see some live music at least once a month (31st December, this year)
3. I fit comfortably into my old jeans (31st December, this year)

You'll notice that they have a deadline assigned to them. Why is that?

A goal without a deadline really isn't anything more than a 'milestone' - something that you plan to pass someday. If a goal is open ended then it's something that you can put off till tomorrow, or the next day, or maybe next week. And putting goals off defeats the object. You might as well start each one with the phrase "Won't it be nice when...?" Whereas if a goal has a deadline then it becomes something you can *fail*.

Contrary to what you may have heard, failure – or more accurately, the fear of failure – isn't necessarily a 'bad thing'. No one likes failing. Failure makes you feel bad. And generally speaking people, even people who wouldn't describe themselves as competitive, will do anything they can to avoid that feeling. Most of the time fear is the very thing that gets us to do something. It raises our heart rate, our pupils dilate and it gets our body ready to "fight" or "take flight".

It makes us do something.

Take my track record, for example. I used to set five goals at the start of each year – three primary, and two in reserve (Call me optimistic!)

At the end of 2008 (my first real year of goal setting) I managed to achieve two.

At the end of 2009 I achieved one. Maybe one and a half.

Last year (2010) I achieved… none.

On the face of it this looks like dismal failure. However, three years later and *all five* of my original five goals have been achieved. So, although I failed to meet the lofty heights I set for myself in the time scales I initially wanted, I did achieve my 2008 goals *eventually.*

You might think that this adds strength to the argument that some goals could be 'open ended'. Especially if the goal itself isn't, strictly speaking, time dependent. Why put yourself under unnecessary pressure? Because the pressure is necessary – the deadline introduces the possibility of failure, and the fear of failure is what drives you to take action.

Have you ever seen the UK TV show 'Grand Designs'? Each week slightly smug but none the less likeable presenter Kevin McCloud follows a couple as they attempt to build their dream house.

"And when do you expect to be moving in?" asks Kevin at the start of each show. To which most couples usually say "Christmas" or "Summer" or "This time next year" or some other date that seems as though it was plucked from thin air. If memory serves me correctly, there's only been one couple who have ever managed to meet their deadline - most have nothing more than a shell of a building when the self-imposed moving in date appears.

However, every now and then Kev meets a couple who waft away his question and tell him that *there is no deadline*, that *it'll happen when it happens*. They usually smile at this point, mentally patting themselves on the back for avoiding the trap of self-imposed pressure and heartache. Forty five minutes later in TV viewing time, and eighteen months or more in real time, they still haven't got anything that even vaguely resembles a house. Instead they're knee deep in mud, living in a leaky caravan, and sharing a portaloo with a dozen slow-moving builders. They're certainly not smiling. And Kevin's smugness has reached new limits.

Setting a goal such as "I have built my dream house" isn't a goal until it has a deadline. Without a deadline you're never in any danger of failing the goal. "I have built my dream house *by the end of the year*" - now that's a goal I can respect, because even if, come December, you only have the foundations built and a big pile of bricks in the corner, at least you have the foundations and a big pile of bricks!

Your goal's deadline is the day you're going to either pat yourself on the back, or give yourself a stern talking to.

It is the day of reckoning.

So to make sure this day doesn't come and go unnoticed you should put it in your diary.

You do have a diary, don't you?

What's wrong?

Feeling some resistance?

Step 5: Add a penalty to your goals
Occasionally the "fear" of failing a goal isn't enough.

My deadline day comes around – and what do ya know, I haven't made my first million, I don't own a yacht in the South of France, and I'm still waiting for Kylie to call. I failed my goals. Big bloomin' deal.

This tends to happen when there really isn't a consequence if the goal isn't met. Life without Kylie or a yacht or a million quid might be a little less exciting than I'd like, but it isn't *unbearable*. The trick therefore is to introduce a penalty.

It took me about six years to write the first draft of my novel. Despite the fact that I dreamt of being a author, and that part of this merely required the ability to sit down and put one word after another, it took an extraordinary amount of effort to motivate myself into doing so. It wasn't that I didn't know what to write, or that I didn't like what I was writing, it was that there was always *tomorrow*.

Even after I made finishing the first draft of my novel a goal (written in the present tense, with a deadline), I still failed dismally. The facts were that the consequence of not writing the novel just didn't hurt enough.

Then one day I decided that I would donate £100 to charity each month I failed to complete a chapter. I couldn't afford £100 a month. Did it work?

No.

A month went by. I wrote nothing and, as a consequence, I donated £100 to charity. It hurt. But it didn't hurt enough.

Then my accountant queried the £100 payment. I told her what I was doing and, being a woman who knows a lot about the movement of money, she told me that the experience of 'doing something good' was offsetting the pain of losing the money. To alleviate this problem she would not only decide who the charity would be, but she would keep that information confidential, and future 'penalty payments' would be made payable to her. She also declared that as she was my accountant I had very little choice in the matter. It was a case of "Do this, or find another accountant."

Another month went by. I wrote nothing. Again.

Then, to my horror, I was duly summoned by my accountant and told I would be taking her to lunch (which I had to pay for) and to bring any completed chapters - or my cheque book. When no chapters were forthcoming I had to write out a cheque for £100. No explanation for my failure was required – indeed, my accountant was quite sympathetic, and I got the distinct impression that she would be quite sympathetic on a monthly basis.

To this day I don't know what charity (if any) the money went to. But I do know this: it was the only time it happened. The first draft of my novel[22] was completed within six months.

---

[22] 'The Good Guy's Guide to Getting Girls.' Despite the title, it is, I assure you, a work of fiction.

Step 6: Add a reward to your goals

Remember we talked about how people fall into two distinct groups? Those that 'run away' from things, and those that 'run towards' things?

A 'running away from' approach to life is great for avoiding sabre tooth tigers. It's also useful when it comes to creating penalties for your goals. Dream up something you really don't want – make that your penalty. Job done.

Every now and then I come across someone from the _other_ group. Someone who naturally 'runs towards things'.

There aren't many of these people around. Presumably most were eaten by sabre tooth tigers many years ago. They're also unlikely to be reading this book given that, in my experience, they're optimistic, have a sunny disposition, and can be quite successful. These people tend to harness the power of focus without even trying which, if I wasn't such a charitable person, I would find distinctly annoying.

They don't, however, respond to penalties at all well. It just doesn't have the same motivating effect, and in some cases it can be crippling. These folks need 'carrots' rather than 'sticks', because sometimes goals, no matter how worthy they may be, just aren't carroty enough.

If you're such a person – if you get excited about the idea of earning a 'gold star' at the end of a task - then go ahead and use the 'penalty' logic in reverse. Dream up a series of treats or rewards and assign them to your goals. Heck, why not do both?

STOP! ACTION POINT!

Re-write your three goals

Rewrite your three goals as follows:
- Positive statements (so that the mind focuses on what you want, not what you don't want)
- Personal statements ("I am.." at the beginning)
- Written in the present tense (it's happening now or has happened)
- Make them measureable (How will you know when the goals have been met?)
- Give your goals a deadline (a realistic deadline – but not one in the far distant future)
- Make a "day of reckoning" appointment with yourself - put the deadline in your diary
- Attach a penalty if you need one
- And maybe a reward

Making Your Goals 'Happen'

Annoyingly, no matter how well written they may be, goals don't achieve themselves.

The first year I set myself goals I failed spectacularly to achieve any of them and for one stupid reason: having set them, I never gave them another thought.

I set five goals on January 1st, and didn't look at them again until January *of the following year*. It took me an entire twelve months to learn the bloomin' obvious: goals don't achieve themselves.

This is basically the same problem with any list you might make – be that a Now List, a to-do list, or even a list of goals. Unless there's a corresponding process in place to make you look at that list and do something with it, the list will remain a list.

Fortunately for you, when it comes to goals, there are plenty of 'processes'. Let's start with a biggy:

Goals Day

Hello? Goals Day? Could this be the slightly more serious cousin of Boxing Day and Now List Day? Well yes. Yes it is.

Your Goals Day is an entire day you set aside, once a month, or every other month - maybe once a week or a fortnight if you can manage it - to work on achieving your goals. This relatively small amount of concentrated effort will make all the difference between achieving and failing your goals.

Now there will be those amongst you who will be gnawing at the corner of this book in frustration (I wouldn't recommend that if you're using an electronic device to read it).

"Another day out of my busy schedule?" you might be saying. "Are you serious?!"

Yes. Yes I am. And whereas I can sort of understand why you'd resist the concept of 'making time to enjoy yourself', working on your three goals shouldn't be a hard sell.

Those three wishes you decided upon a couple of pages back, and spent time crafting into the most powerful goals you could come up with, they should - in some way - reflect the three things you want most in life. If they don't then you haven't got the right goals! But assuming you've identified three goals that'll rock your world, or at the very least make it a darn sight more enjoyable, anything that gets in the way of your goals should be, by its very nature, less important.

Yes, most of us have to work, most of us have responsibilities, but 12 days out of a possible 341[23] is still a slither over 3.5%. You spend ten times that amount of time asleep! You probably spend more than 12 days per year just sitting on the toilet! Now that's a sobering thought.

If you seriously can't commit a whole day once a month, then commit half a day, or one day every other month. Or maybe an hour each day. Whatever works for you. And if you are in this situation then I seriously recommend creating a goal to regain control of your life! (Suggested goal: "I am able

---

[23] 12 days have already been taken by Boxing Day, and another 12 by Now List Day

to dedicate one day a month to working on my goals (31st Dec, this year)")

But before we fall out over your insanely busy schedule let me sell you some of the benefits. Whilst Goals Day isn't necessarily 'fun' (it feels more like work), it does nonetheless give you a fantastic sense that you're taking control of your life and doing something about it. A day spent on goals is hugely empowering. It's rare that I don't finish a Goals Day feeling like my life has been nudged forward just that little bit more, sometimes a lot more. For that feeling alone it's worth the investment.

Rules of Goals Day

There are, of course, some rules:

Firstly, your Goals Day should be a regular occurrence. Presently I only manage to have a Goals Day once a month – I'd prefer once a fortnight. But if I had a Goals Day less than once a month I'd start to get seriously jittery.

By 'regular' I also mean 'planned'. Once again you should make an appointment with yourself. In your computerised diary/calendar (now, you do have a diary… don't you?), create a new appointment and set it to repeat every X days/month.

Secondly, what happens when Goals Day coincides with your significant other's birthday? What then? Cancel Goals Day? No no no no no... as with Boxing Days and Now List Days you can reschedule a Goals Day, but you can't cancel it. If this means that by the end of the year you have 12 Goals

Days all stacked up next to each other, well that's unfortunate, but so be it.

What actually happens on a Goals Day?

Let's have a quick recap on what Goals Day is supposed to be about.

This is a day set aside for doing whatever you can to nudge one or two of your goals further.

You might like to split the day into two - work one goal in the morning, and a different goal in the afternoon. This isn't a hard and fast rule, and it might be something that you want to play by ear, but working on one goal all day long can be draining to say the least.

And for some of you that's pretty much all you need to know to kick off a blur of frantic list making. Those people will start building 'Gantt charts', they'll know what the 'milestones' are, and what should and shouldn't be on the 'critical path', and they'll have already decided who's going to be blamed when the 'deliverables' fail to be... well... delivered. The rest of you won't have a clue what I'm talking about.

I could write a huge section on how to break each of your goals down into smaller chunks, and how to work out what those chunks might be - but someone far more skilled than me has already done it.

If you can, get hold of a copy of 'Getting Things Done'[24] by David Allen.

---

[24] ISBN-13: 978-0749922641

'Getting Things Done' is a practical, easy to follow, no nonsense guide for creating a structure in your life to *move things forward*. If someone decided to sit down and write the 'handbook for human productivity' this would be it.

It's had a hugely positive influence on my life, albeit in a very simple, no nonsense way. It's one of those books that I keep having to buy over and over again because the friends I lend it to *never* give it back. That's how good it is! And I wish I'd written it first.

Right now on Amazon.co.uk I can see that there are at least a dozen (second hand paperback) copies on sale for less than a fiver – trust me, it's well worth that and the delivery charge you'll pay.

However, whilst you're waiting for the postman to bring you your copy, let me lift one tiny piece of advice from Mr Allen's excellent book and share it with you now.

To achieve anything there are always a finite number of steps between where you are, and where you want to be. And whilst it can be useful to know what these steps are, or might be, it isn't always necessary. Sometimes all you need to know is '*what should I do next?*'

So if you're sitting there on Goals Day, looking at your goals and wondering what on earth you should be doing, ask yourself that question. For each of the goals you want to work on, what would be 'the next step'?

If several answers come to mind, jot them all down on a piece of paper, then set about doing the one that seems the most logical. If that leads you nowhere, go back to your list and try the next idea.

If no answers come to mind then may I humbly suggest that the 'thing you should do next', is find someone who can tell you.

For instance, my good friend Karen recently decided that she was going to set about realising her long term dream of opening a Therapy Life Centre. She set herself a goal. Booked in some Goal Days... and promptly got stuck.

"What," she thought, "do I do next?"

Her solution was to invite me and some friends round for a brainstorming session. By the end of that afternoon she had a pretty clear idea of what she had to do to make the centre a reality.

Whilst I might not be available for a similar brainstorming session in your house I'm willing to bet that, with a little searching, you can find someone who's either done what you want to do, or would have some ideas on how to go about it.

So, ready to start achieving those goals and changing your life? Let's do it:

STOP! ACTION POINT!

Consider booking regular Goals Days into your diary

Remember:
- ➢ You can move it – but you can't cancel it
- ➢ On your Goals Day, you may like to work one goal in the morning, and a different goal in the afternoon

Goal Minutes

Whilst Goals Days are extremely powerful, they're not the complete answer. They're maybe 57% of the answer. And whilst your goals are probably very different to my goals, personally it would be utterly impossible to achieve just one of my goals with only 12 days' effort a year, regardless of how concerted that effort was. It takes more than that. Much more.

Fortunately though, I don't necessarily need more time in the form of *days*. Sometimes I just need an extra five minutes, but an extra five minutes at *just the right moment*. Sometimes I just need those 5 minutes when I'm at a party and find myself talking to someone who, if I just remember to ask them the right questions, could be the very person I've been looking for to help me build that new website. Or maybe I need those five minutes when I'm walking past the local adult education centre when for weeks I've been meaning to phone up and ask someone to send me an evening class prospectus. Opportunities like this happen more often than you think – you just have to be able to spot them when they happen.

Remember how we talked earlier about 'focus' and how the brain works? How, when you've decided what car you're going to buy, you suddenly start seeing that same car everywhere? These next couple of steps are designed to tap into that part of your brain and keep your mind focused on your goals so that when those crucial five minutes appear, you spot them and spring into action.

To do this we're simply going to review our goals. Every single day. Sometimes several times a day. Without fail. If that sounds onerous, fastidious, perhaps even slightly compulsive, relax. It's far easier than you think.

Got a wallet?

Most people own a wallet, or purse, or some other item to carry around their payment cards, dog-eared receipts or, if you're really retro, cash.

If your wallet is like mine then it might have a small see-through pocket where you're supposed to put a photo of a loved one. Ditch it. Not the loved one, just the photo.

On a small piece of card or paper, just big enough to fit that space, write down all your goals or, if they won't fit onto such a tiny piece of card (they probably won't), the one that's most important to you, and place it in your wallet. What we're trying to do here is create something that will remind you of your goal each and every time you look in your wallet.

(If you can't bring yourself to ditch the photo then see if you can engineer it so that the photo and your goal reminder share the space – in truth, that's what I've done).

This is a very simple idea but one that really works.

You might be tempted to think "I don't need to do this – there's no way I can forget what my number 1 goal is." But you're missing the point. This idea, and the ones that follow, aren't some sort of 'aide memoire' – it's much more subtle than that. What we're creating is your own personal *subliminal advertising campaign*. We're going to bombard your subconscious with images and reminders so that the 'focus' mechanism in your head is permanently on the lookout for anything that applies to your goals.

So imagine you're standing at the bar, paying for a drink. As you reach for your money your eyes register the small piece of card with your number one goal written on it. "My polo shirt business has doubled its turnover. 31st Dec. This year." You take out a twenty pound note and hand it to the barman, at which point you notice that his polo shirt has the name of the pub chain embroidered on the breast. I wonder where they get their polo shirts from, you think to yourself.

"Here ya go, mate," says the barman as he hands you your change.

"Thanks," you say. "By the way – have you got a telephone number for your head office?"

Got a 'Primary Location'?

Most of us spend our days in just one or two locations. Whether that's a desk, the inside of a delivery van, your spot next to the conveyer belt, or your kitchen and home, a significant portion of your day is probably spent in just one place. Wherever that may be you can take the general principle of the 'card in the wallet' idea and make a bigger, more elaborate version to suit the space you work in.

What you come up with will, of course, depend on you and your primary location. So if you spend most of your days at home you might like to take a large sheet of coloured paper, write your goals on it in big colourful letters, and stick it to the fridge. If you have young kids - and especially if your goals are shared by the whole family - you could get them to help you decorate it. (My niece never needs much encouragement to get up to her elbows in glue and glitter!) On the other hand, if your kids are older (or you can't be bothered with all that mess), buy some magnetic letters and spell your goal out on the fridge door.

If you're very creative and practical, you might like to make something you can put in a picture frame; something that you can put on a desk or hang somewhere prominent.

If you're less hands-on, but own a computer, you could use it to find a picture on the internet (maybe via a Google image search) that sums up (one of) your goals, then use whatever software you have (maybe Photoshop, or PowerPoint) to add your goal's text on top of it. For example:

Once you've done this there are *numerous* web-based services that, for a few pence (really, pence!), will turn your image into a poster (for your college bedroom), a key ring (to hang in the van, or put your keys on), a mouse mat (for your work desk), postcards (to put inside your locker), even a handbag! Wherever you work there really isn't an excuse for not having some kind of imagery to remind you of your goal(s), frequently, throughout the day.

Whilst you're sitting at your computer, what's your computer background (the wallpaper) of choice? A sunset? A picture of your dog? Dear God, I hope it's not the Windows or Apple logo. Why not use that image you just created? In fact, why not make an image for each of your goals and then use something like 'webshots' (a very cool, totally free piece of software available from webshots.com) to change it daily?

Personally, I go one step further and use Windows Scheduled Task manager to open my three wallpaper images so that they are the first thing I see when I switch on my computer monitor.

Obviously, if you work alongside other people and your goals are very personal, or you're just a very private person, these ideas might not appeal to you. There are two things I'd say about that. Firstly, to preserve your modesty try creating something that will remind you of your goal, but without using any words – just imagery. So long as you know what the image represents the effect on your subconscious will be the same. Secondly, so what if your colleagues know! If they're nice colleagues I encourage you to let them in on your goals. Trust me, nothing motivates you more than knowing you've got to give a progress report every time someone sees that image on your desk.

Either way, do this right and pretty soon you won't be able to go through your day without your computer, fridge, locker, or wall gently reminding your subconscious what to focus on.

But we haven't finished yet. Your eyes aren't the only way to absorb information.

Got ears?

In the last section I suggested getting into the habit of reciting your top three wishes (which have now been re-written as goals, making them all the more powerful) as you walk up the stairs, blow dry your hair, drive to work, or something else you have to do every day.

Now there will be those amongst you, my fellow self-help book junkies, who will recognise that what I'm really talking about here are "affirmations".

Affirmations (sometimes portrayed in movies as a guy standing in front of a mirror repeating phrases like "I am successful, *I am successful*") cause many people to raise an eyebrow – people either love them or hate them. I used to be firmly in the latter group.

However, remember how I mentioned that your subconscious is very suggestible? That if it's told something frequently enough, it will eventually believe it? Which in turn will have a knock-on effect on your behaviour and the choices you make? Interestingly, this includes all the times <u>you</u> tell <u>yourself</u> that *you're stupid, you don't feel well*, or *you don't like something*. There's been a surprising amount of research on the subject of 'self-talk' and it turns out that negative internal chatter is far more damaging than you might think.

Recently a big dirty ginger cat moved into my neighbourhood. It's a nasty looking brute. It's the kind of cat that scowls and looks as if it should be wearing an eye patch.

But worse than that, it's taken a particular dislike to CJ. My cat.

For several weeks now I've had a water pistol at the back door ready for the moments when I hear CJ hurtle through the cat flap with Evil Ginger Cat in hot pursuit. The last time this happened was about two o'clock this morning. I was woken by the now familiar sounds of two cats either side of a plastic flap, batting it back and forth with their claws and paws whilst they hiss and howl at each other. I grabbed my robe, ran down the stairs, grabbed my water pistol and, as I opened the back door, fired off two shots into the darkness.

When I poked my head outside I could just see the shadowy image of the ginger cat, silhouetted at the end of the garden, just out of firing range. But I was ready for him. I reached into the bucket by the back door and grabbed one of the water-filled balloons that I'd prepared for this very moment, and I lobbed it with all my might in his general direction.

As I did so, I felt my ring - my wedding ring - slide off my finger, and a second or so later I heard it tinkle on the paving slabs, somewhere in the garden. In the darkness.

This morning, when the sun eventually came up, I went into the garden and spent a good half hour looking for the darn thing. A small silver coloured ring, against small grey slabs, covered with a layer of dead leaves, in the rain and the bitter cold. Not surprisingly, my hopes of ever finding my one and only sentimental piece of jewellery weren't high, and as I worked my way from one end of the garden to the other and back again, I muttered the words, "I'm never going to find this thing," under my breath.

Now this is the God's honest truth, but eventually I realised what I was doing - telling my mind that I would not find the ring! So I changed the words. "I *am* going to find my ring." I said it once. Then again. And again – and as I carried on looking, within about five seconds (I managed to say the phrase to myself about five times) I found it! I was so surprised I actually spent a few seconds checking the engraving inside the ring just in case I'd found a completely different platinum wedding ring amongst the leaves in my garden.

Coincidence? Maybe. I'd go as far to say probably. But then I've seen hypnotists persuade people that they can't see what's clearly right in front of their eyes.

The facts are the brain merely interprets the information coming in through our senses, and as we're in control of our brains, we're in control of that interpretation process.

Negative self-talk is a *really* bad habit to get into. And given that there's often a queue of people lining up to point out our faults, why be one of them?

Instead, I encourage you to become your own fan club and use self-talk (affirmations) to your advantage. When you say your goals to yourself, say them out loud. Say them several times. Say them like you mean it.

You may find it easier to remember what to say (and the fact that you have to say them at all), if you have them pinned to the mirror, or the dashboard, or the bottom of the stairs. Personally, I read them out loud when I switch on my computer screen each morning.

More powerful still is to record your affirmations, then play them back to yourself each day, and repeat what you hear. This prevents you from rushing through your daily affirmations. If you're musical, put them to music, but if you're like the rest of us, just read them slowly and clearly into a tape recorder.

If you own an iPod or other MP3 player, and have the ability on your computer to record your voice, you could go the whole hog and create yourself an "audio screensaver" - a thirty second audio snippet that pops up now and again and reminds you of your goals. It's a little like having a motivational commercial break whilst you're listening to your fave tunes.

Here's how:

1. Record yourself reading the goals and create an MP3 file. Keep it short: 30 seconds or so. I usually read through my 5 goals twice.
2. Import into your iTunes[25] music library.
3. Set up your MP3 player (I use the 'playlist' functionality in iTunes) so that your 'self-talk' file appears periodically. I have a 'driving' playlist that I use in the car that always includes my self-talk file.
4. Create a rule with yourself that you will not skip this file when it plays if you're the only one who can hear it.
5. When the file plays, if you're alone, repeat the goals out loud to yourself.

Now there are those of you out there who will have decided that I've just gone too far and I'm clearly bonkers. You're not

---

[25] Or equivalent

alone. My brother was stunned into silence when I told him about this, which, if you know my brother, you'll know is a rare thing indeed. But believe me, it works. Whether you use 'impromptu iPod affirmation sessions' or you merely recite your goals every morning, by using self-talk you're giving your psyche something positive to work with.[26]

---

[26] An excellent book on the subject of affirmations and self-talk is: 'What to Say When You Talk to Your Self', by Shad Helmstetter. ISBN-13: 978-0722525111

STOP! ACTION POINT!

Use the power of focus by creating a subliminal advertising campaign for your subconscious

Try any or all of these ideas:
➢ Put a reminder of your goals or primary goal in the photo part of your wallet or purse
➢ Create images applicable to your goals and place them where you will see them during the course of each day
➢ Use affirmations. Say your five goals out loud to yourself each day. Record them to make the experience more powerful

Find yourself a Goal Partner

Right after Goal Days, and filling your life with subliminal (and less than subliminal) reminders of your goals, having a Goals Partner is probably the next most effective way of achieving your goals.

My Goals Partner is Denny. In fact, Denny was the one who got me interested in the concept of goal setting in the first place. If you're not enjoying this part of the book then Denny's to blame. At least in part.

Let me reiterate something – Denny was the one who got me *interested* in goals. She didn't introduce the concept to me. Having read more than my fair share of self help books I thought I knew all that I needed to know about goal setting – enough to know that it wasn't for me – but Denny was the first one who made it fun.

"I've set myself 5 goals for next year," she told me one winter's night in January, over a curry.

"You've set yourself goals?" I said

"Yeah," said Denny, mopping up some curry sauce with a strip of naan bread. I was stunned.

"Why?" I asked.

"Because I'm fed up with my life being like it is."

"Setting yourself goals is a little extreme though, isn't it?" She shrugged.

"Not really," she said.

"But what if you don't achieve them?" I asked.

"Then life will stay pretty much as it is, I guess. From that perspective I can't really lose." I thought about this for a second or two.

"Maybe I should set some goals," I said.

"Maybe you should," said Denny. "What would they be?" For the rest of the meal we chatted about what each of our goals would be, and why. It was fun. And that made a huge difference – setting my goals with someone else was *fun*. It wasn't some crazy thing I was doing on my own. It didn't feel like I was working in a vacuum. But more to the point, now someone else knew about my goals and would hold me accountable.

This same technique is used by clinics to help people quit smoking. Merely knowing that there's someone out there who knows that you've made a commitment to yourself increases your chances of success dramatically.

One word of warning. The first year Denny and I set our goals we didn't check how each other was doing until the following year. That was a missed opportunity. Especially as we meet for a curry at least once a month. Now we quiz each other on our goals progress each and every time we pay a visit to the curry house. It doesn't necessarily dominate the conversation, but it's as much a part of the curry experience as ordering poppadoms, or the hot towels at the end.

STOP! ACTION POINT!

Consider finding yourself a Goals Partner

Got a friend out there who'd be happy to be your Goals Partner? Give 'em a call. Invite them over for a meal. Lend them this book if you have to[27]. Once you've persuaded them, remember to:
- ➤ Meet up regularly to discuss your goals
- ➤ Keep it fun

---

[27] Lend? What am I saying!? <u>Buy</u> them a copy!

The Day Of Reckoning

Breaking open the champagne!

Hopefully you've actually achieved one or two of your goals. Maybe, just maybe, all three?

Let's consider that for a moment. You've achieved something that was *so important to you* it was amongst the top three on your original Wish List, and was subsequently made into a goal! Well, big pat on the back for you! Congratulations! You should celebrate. Seriously - you should. It creates positive reinforcement in your psyche. The better the celebration, the more you'll want to achieve future goals.

So, having achieved a goal, does that somehow prevent you from making a new one to replace it? Of course not! You're on a roll – dig out that Wish List and write yourself a new goal to replace the one you've just achieved.

And this time, dare to think bigger. Much bigger.

Oh, and feel free to skip the next couple of pages.

What's up? Why are you still here? Why the long face?

Oh.

I see.

Close, but no cigar...

So, you failed one of your goals.

Maybe two of them?

All three?

I'm sorry to hear that – though not as sorry as you might expect.

So what happens now? Should you declare the whole 'goals' experiment a disaster and have a ritual burning of this book? Definitely not! Not when you could re-sell this book on Amazon. No, get rid of this book if you must, but if you give up on goals now you've only done half the work.

Firstly: You failed, but you're not a failure
This is important: whilst you failed to achieve the goal, if you made time to work on your goals, and if you moved yourself forward even one inch, you, the person, are *not* 'a failure'.

'Failures' are people who don't get out of bed in the morning. 'Failures' are people who don't even try. But each and every time you worked on your goals you were achieving something, so let's not start branding ourselves with a big fat F, because as we already know, that kind of negative self-talk is toxic and unhelpful.

Let me reiterate this:

YOU FAILED TO ACHIEVE THE GOAL, BUT YOU ARE NOT A FAILURE.

Secondly: You're supposed to fail (more times than you succeed)!
The not so funny thing about setting goals is that some of the time, perhaps even *most of the time*, you *should* fail!

This could just be me but I'm not particularly motivated by 'easy goals' – goals that I know I have a good chance of achieving. They don't even feel like goals - more like boring items on my to-do list.

I had a friend who, on January 1^{st,} set herself the goal of joining a gym. By the end of the first week she'd achieved it. Was that really a goal? Was that really one of her *top three* items on her Wish List? Shouldn't joining the gym have been part of a much larger goal to improve her health and fitness?

In my mind a goal should stretch you. A goal should be ever-so-slightly out of reach. With most of my goals I know that my chances of success are extremely slim, though the chance is there.

You don't have to succeed first time!

A lot of people have this inbuilt drive to succeed, *first time*. What a terrifying prospect! There are very few things in life where you're only allowed to have one attempt.

And - whether you're learning to drive, learning to paint, running a marathon, overcoming your fear of approaching women - whilst it hurts to fail, there isn't actually anything physical preventing you from trying again. And again. And again.

It depends on the goal but in general I'm not particularly keen on *succeeding first time*. There's very little to be learnt from a first time success – I'd rather fail but know how close I got, and why.

Which brings us rather nicely onto the next and *most important* point about failure.

Failure is 'feedback'

You can learn a lot from failing. Sometimes it's just a new way of *not* doing something. Other times it's that you need more time. And if you take that information and use it to help you make better decisions, to try a different approach, to increase your chances of success, was it really failure? This might be a hard thing to comprehend, but that 'failure' can be a very good thing *if* you treat it properly.

The most important aspect of failure is the new information it gives you.

So, grab yourself some paper and ask yourself the following questions:

1. Why did I fail? Did I run out of time? Or was there another reason?
2. What have I achieved? Would I have done so without this goal in place?
3. What do I need to achieve this goal? More time? Something else?
4. Is this goal still relevant? Does it need re-writing? Should it be replaced with a different goal?

The answers to these questions serve to do three things:
1. They should console you – by concentrating on what you have achieved
2. They should inform you – by identifying the reasons why you failed
3. They should inspire you – so you know how to set subsequent goals

In many ways the concepts of success and failure are far too rigid, far too black and white, far too binary. Maybe you weren't 100% successful – but were you 80%? 50%? 25%?

'Real failure', so they say, is not 'the falling down'. Real failure is 'not getting up again'.

Now, pick yourself up – and start again.

But the word "failure"- arrgggghhh!!!

My assistant was the first person to read this book and she suggested I find another word for 'failure'.

"It's such a negative word," she said. "It implies you tried but weren't 'good enough'. Can't you tell them that there is no failure - they just didn't, well, 'achieve it'? The word failure makes me itch!"

It makes you itch, eh? Now that is interesting. Tell me more about this itch. Is it annoying? Does it make you feel uncomfortable? Does it make you want to wriggle about? Do whatever you can to get rid of it?

No one likes failure. When we fail it causes us pain. I've watched my six year old nephew throw objects across a room in frustration when he lost a game of Snakes and Ladders. The experience of failure is so upsetting that many people develop a fear of failure.

Fear, pain and, indeed, itching, are all mechanisms your body uses to motivate you. Surely anything that motivates you is, at least in part, useful?

Resetting Your Goals

What? You thought goals setting was a one time deal?
'Au contraire' my friend, 'au contraire'.

By identifying why you achieved or failed your goals
you're equipped to write smarter, more specific, or maybe
utterly different goals. But the important thing is to cash in on
all that new information and make better ones.

Avoid, if you can, simply resetting an old goal. The
definition of 'insanity', so they say, is trying the same thing
over and over and expecting a different result. But by now
you should have lots of new information to feed into the Goal
setting process.

Take for instance one of my goals for 2010:

**MY HAPPINESS BOOK IS PUBLISHED
(DEC 31ST 2010)**

At the time that I set the Goal, I'd hardly started writing
the book, let alone given much thought to how I would
publish it. Now, not only do I know what I need to do to get
this into your hands, but I also have a pretty good idea of
where I want to go after that. So my revised Goal for 2011
looks something like this:

"HOW TO DO EVERYTHING AND BE HAPPY"
IS AVAILABLE IN THREE FORMATS,
AND SELLING REALLY WELL (TO BE DEFINED),
WHILST I BASK IN THE SUCCESS (TO BE DEFINED)
OF THE SEMINAR(S)[28]
DEC 31ST 2011

I like to set my goals at the start of each year, and review them at the end. For me, that works. This might make them sound a little like 'resolutions' but resolutions are something entirely different. "I will give up smoking" - that's a resolution. "I have given up smoking (Dec, this year)" - now that's a goal.

You don't have to set them yearly. Maybe quarterly works for you. Maybe it's dependent on your goals. The important thing is not how often you review or renew them, *it's that you do*.

Working with goals – that is, having them in your life – is something that gets easier the longer you do it. You develop a habit, or a mindset – after a while you start to look at everything you're doing in relation to how it sits with your goals. In a very real way, your goals force you to decide what's important to you and move you in that direction. They give you purpose and vision.

It's true what they say:

"WITHOUT VISION THE PEOPLE PERISH."

---

[28] Find out more about the seminars at www.howtodoeverythingandbehappy.com

STOP! ACTION POINT!

The Day of Reckoning

If you fail a goal
...ask yourself the following:

1. Why did I fail? Did I run out of time? Or was there another reason?
2. What *have* I achieved? Would I have done so without this goal in place?
3. What do I need to achieve this goal? More time? Something else?
4. Is this goal still relevant? Does it need re-writing? Should it be replaced with a different goal?

If you achieve a goal
...congratulations! Go back to your Wish List, or create a new one, and set yourself a new goal.
This time, think bigger.

Use all this information to set new goals.

Potential Goal Problems

Ok, settle down, settle down –from experience I already know that there are probably 50% of you out there who are sitting, arms folded tightly across your chest, scowling at me. Of all the concepts discussed in this book goal setting is the one that people wrestle with most.

So, whilst I suspect this section of the book will probably turn into a work in progress (maybe check the website for updates: www.howtodoeverythingandbehappy.com) let me try and address as many of those common goal-related problems as possible.

Words and terminology
"Goals", "wishes", "failure" – some people have a real problem with these words:

"Goals" sounds too corporate, too managerial, too board-room, too annoying, too school teacher-ish...

"Wishes" sounds too flaky, too holy, too hippy, too girly...

And let's not get started on "failure"! We already know how that brings some people out in hives!

If you're struggling with these, or any other words, then *change them*. Pick something else. You have my permission to go through your copy of the book and change the word "goal" to "target" – or "wish" to "desire," or whatever you like. Whatever works for you. The important thing is not *the word*, but the concept behind it, so if you can't hear "failure" without wanting to scratch, *change it* to something else – how about "Personal Target Re-assessment Opportunity"?!

If you think of any good word alternatives feel free to send them to me and I'll list them on the website for your fellow word-challenged readers, but please, don't let a word stop you from getting the most out of goal setting or this book.

Too American
It's important to realise that I am British. True - I don't live in a castle, I don't have a butler, I don't particularly like battered fish wrapped in newspaper, I'm not a huge fan of roast beef, I can't stand 'soccer', but other than that, most of the stereotypes are probably accurate.

I have worked for numerous American companies over the past fifteen years and some of their culture may have rubbed off on me – some. But I've *never* skipped my lunch, worked late into the night, high-fived my colleagues, or winked at them whilst saying, "Good job!"

That said, our 'cousins' across the pond are, as a nation, just a whole lot better at 'self-improvement' than we Brits are. And for decades American authors have taken ideas that work, re-branded them, and presented them to the book-buying public as groundbreaking and new. So if you've ever read, watched or heard anything on 'goal setting' or 'the Law of Attraction' it's possible that the ideas presented in this book are going to feel – well, 'American'.

So here's a suggestion: join me. Join my little crusade to reclaim these sensible, practical, powerful ideas and re-present them, without the fluff, without the mystique, and with a distinctly European flavour.

I just don't have the time!
Hang on - didn't I address this way back at the start of the
book? And then again under Now Lists? And yet some of you
are still convinced that to apply everything you've learnt in
this book you've somehow got to conjure up 36 days out of
thin air, which you've already decided is totally impossible.

And so it is.

Let me be clear on this point:

**YOU DO NOT NEED TO
FIND 36 DAYS
TO MAKE THIS BOOK WORK.**

What's needed here is a little creative 'time accountancy'
and 'labelling'. We're going to take all the important things
you're *currently* doing and shuffle them around to fit one of
the three days mentioned in this book. We're going to re-
organise.

So let's recap what each of the days are and how you can
fit them into your oh-so-busy life.

Boxing Days - Boxing Day can usually be 'reclaimed'
from activities, particularly weekend activities, that have only
filled your time up till now because there was nothing else
planned. Some people get up on Saturday and spend it
shopping or washing the car or watching football on the TV,
and for no other reason than it's Saturday! If that's you, one
Saturday a month can now become Boxing Day. And if you
wake up on that Boxing Day and you *want* to go shopping, or
watch the match, then go ahead.

Now List Days – These don't have to be whole days. Not if you're planning. You can break them down and have Now List evenings, lunchtimes, even breakfasts. And if you're not *planning* – if you're actually ready to do an item on your list – that might be a perfect vacation activity rather than spending another day sitting around the pool[29].

Goal Days - Goal Days are twelve measly days out of 365 to be spent on the three things that you want most of all in life.
Let me say that again:
The three things you want <u>MOST OF ALL</u>!

Before you bought this book one of two things was happening. Either you were completely ignoring all the things that are now on your Wish List, in which case you were probably deeply unhappy or, more likely, you *were* struggling to address those three things, albeit in your own way.
Long before I discovered the power of goals I spent many an evening and weekend struggling to turn my writing and other interests into something that might bring in a few quid. If you've been doing the same then all that time you currently spend working on your dreams and ambitions can now be *reallocated* as Goal Days (or evenings, weekends etc). Maybe it's not 12 *days* a year – maybe it isn't that structured – but it's

---

[29] Of course, if 'sitting around the pool' is really important to you, add it to your Now List or Wish List.

time that you don't have to 'find'. All you need to do is start using it properly.

I understand that you're busy. I do. And I appreciate that if you work for someone else, and/or you're a parent, you probably can't juggle your diary quite as effectively as I can. I get that. But whilst I've never been a parent, I wasn't always self employed. And whilst life is hardly fair at the best of times, one thing that does seem to be consistent is that anything worth having in this world usually comes at a price. And it's usually a lot more expensive than you initially thought. Happiness is one of those things. To get it you have to work. Hard!

But before I bust your chops any further, here's a suggestion that my friend Wendy came up with.

If you find yourself struggling to juggle your time, perhaps this is a good opportunity to look at what's currently eating up all your minutes.

In Wendy's case, a considerable amount of her day was spent working through what appeared to be an ever growing pile of ironing, until one day she made the momentous decision that, as there were things in life more important than ironing, ironing was no longer going to be a daily activity. Furthermore, if her three teenage children and partner disagreed, then they were welcome to assist whenever they wanted.

Too rigid!

One of the problems with writing a book like this – one that's based heavily upon personal experience – is that all the ideas and suggestions will work perfectly, if you happen to be me.

Of course, you're not me. So when it comes to goal setting (or indeed anything else in this book), for goodness sake use your noodle. If setting *yearly* goals doesn't work for you, set them at other times! One of my friends sets them as and when her life dictates.

If three goals is too many, try two. Or one. If you have enough bandwidth to cope with more than three try four, or five.

And though I've said it already I'll say it again – if I come across a like a school teacher, then I sincerely apologise. I'm just passionate about this stuff. And the more I see it working for people, the more passionate I become.

Oi! I thought you were going to address the difference
between my Wish List and my Now List?

Ah yes. Thanks for reminding me. Let's recap.

You remember we were questioning the difference between your Now List and your Wish List and whether it's ok if something makes both lists – well, now that we've talked about goals lets think about this again.

The short answer is no, it doesn't matter. If you want to put something on both lists and that makes sense to you, go right ahead. What goes on which list is far less important than understanding how each list works and why.

Imagine you head up a corporation with two groups of people at your disposal. Over there, in the factory building, you have your Now List Department, whereas over here, on the fourteenth floor of your corporate headquarters you have the Wish List & Goal Division.

The Now List folks will diligently work through anything and everything you give them, albeit at their own methodical pace, trying to get as many things done before - well, before they run out of time.

The Wish & Goals operatives, on the other hand, will *consider* any request you throw at them, but until it's passed rigorous internal scrutiny to see whether it should be adopted as one of your corporation's three goals, won't do very much with it. When it *is* a goal however, they'll assign a deadline, introduce rewards and penalties, create a poster campaign, organise affirmation sessions, and throw every resource they have at it.

So then, let's take that wish you had earlier to climb Mount Kilimanjaro. Which group of your people do you want to give that to?

Final 'Wish List and Goal' Thoughts

Whilst you have choices (and there are *always* choices, if you look hard enough) you can make changes.

Maybe not everything, and maybe not overnight, but given enough time and consistent effort you can move the mountain of your life from where it stands now to where you want it to be or, at the very least, a good deal closer.

It was Benjamin Disraeli, British Prime Minister, who said, "Success is entirely dependent upon constancy of purpose". He was so right.

Figure out what you want, set yourself goals, and begin.

You can change your life.

Putting It All Together

You've almost finished the book!

Yes, I know – you were hoping that this was an index or the acknowledgements section, or something else you could skip.

Well, if your life has become a blur of Boxing Days, Now Lists, Wish Lists and goal related activity – congratulations! - you probably don't need to read this section. My work here is done.

If, however, you need a little more help and a few pointers on where you should go from here – this section is for you.

Grab a pen and lots of paper.

For real, this time.

What Do You Want?

Start thinking about what you really want, in all areas of your life.

Make Lists

Make the following three lists:

Your Now List

Your Now List is a 'work in progress' list that contains all the things you'd like to experience "before you die". Don't wait until you have an idea before you start this list – the very act of creating a blank list will start your brain thinking of things to put on it.

Your Wish List

Your Wish List is another 'work in progress' list, this time containing all the things you want in your life, or you want your life to be. Think about every aspect of your life – work, personal, spiritual, physical – everything. Think big. Think small. If you have wishes that are reliant or related to each other write those down too. There's no limit on the number of wishes you can have – they merely have to comply with the laws of physics. Go crazy. Write down absolutely everything.

Your Goals List

Your Goals List is very short. It consists only of your top three, most important wishes, re-written in the form of goals.

Focus and Evidence

Having started your lists reinforce the ideas by feeding your subconscious.

Collect inspirational pictures
Spend some time (though not too much time) trawling the internet, or flicking through magazines for any images that inspire you or remind you of things you want.

Mementoes and souvenirs
Out having fun with friends? Keep a paper napkin, pick up a card when you pay the bill, and hold onto that ticket stub. Having the best vacation ever? Send *yourself* a postcard! Pick up a pebble from the beach. Collect anything that can act as evidence of all the times you've enjoyed yourself.

Tools of your trade

There are a variety of objects that you might need to help organise all this list making and collecting activity. They are:
- A couple of cork boards – for inspirational imagery, and your "year board"
- A printer's tray - for items you can't pin to the board
- Image software - to make wallpapers and screensavers
- Sound software - to record affirmation MP3s
- A diary

You do own a diary, don't you?

Making It Happen!

You didn't think I'd finish this book without another diary mention, did you? And there was me thinking we've got to know each other so well.

Create your 'Days'

Grab your diary and put the following appointments in it:

Boxing Day

Maybe once a month – whatever works for you - perhaps the 26th of each month (there's a wacky idea).

Don't worry too much about diary clashes for the moment – you'll sort those out later. Right now it's more important that Boxing Day is in your diary on a regular basis.

Now List Day

Or Now List half day, or lunchtime, or breakfast, or whatever works for you, as regularly as you deem it necessary.

Remember, this is the day when you'll either be doing something on your Now List, or doing things towards making those things happen.

Again, don't worry too much about diary clashes at the moment.

Goals Days

Have Goals Days once a month – or twice if you can. Goals Days are perhaps the most important out of the three different types of day and these are the days that'll ultimately make the biggest impact in your life.

Other Days

Having introduced this concept of pre-arranged 'days', you *might* want to experiment with creating days of your own. This is particularly powerful if you work for yourself, but I've known colleagues who do the same with their working day at Mega Corp Ltd. Here are some days that currently feature in my diary (remember, these are only examples – they may not work for you):

Default Day

Default Days are days specifically set aside for my 'default' activities which are:

- ➢ clearing the post and in-tray,
- ➢ then my email inbox,
- ➢ before returning to the master to-do list.

I try and have a default day once a week. Like all 'days', default days can be moved, but never cancelled.

On the rare occasions that I wake up and find that there's a blank space in my diary I treat it as an extra default day.

Writing Day

Writing Day is the day when I do whatever writing or editing needs to be done. That probably sounds obvious, but because writing is something that I need to 'get into' (it's difficult to dip in and out of writing), it's also one of those tasks which I have a tendency to put off. When 'write the next chapter' appears on my regular to-do list I have a tendency to look at the item below it and say to myself "I'll just do xyz first" rather than sit my bum down and write. Hence Writing Day.

Maybe your equivalent would be a Cleaning Day, or an Admin Day, or Personal Finances Day.

Promo Day

A large part of what I do actually involves promoting my writing and other activities. Promotion is one of those activities which doesn't seem to reap any immediate dividends – for this reason it's extremely easy to leave it till tomorrow as 'one day is unlikely to make a huge difference'.

Unfortunately tomorrow – as the song says – never actually arrives, so the promo work never gets done. For this reason I invented Promo Day.

I soon found that an entire day of promotional activities was too much to cope with, so Promo Day is now a half day, twice a month.

Recovery Day

Recovery Days are inserted as and when I think I'll need them. For instance, if I know I'm going to be flying home from a trip, or having a particularly boozy late night, the following day might be allocated as a Recovery Day.

This might seem extraordinarily decadent. How luxurious that I can afford to take an entire day to recover from a social event! However, too many Writing Days, Promo Days, Goal Days etc were effectively being lost due to trying to operate with a head full of porridge. It seems far more sensible to accept the fact that I need to recharge.

Things still happen on Recovery Day. It's just given over to doing all the mundane tasks that require very little brain power or physical exertion.

Friends and Family

To ensure that Peter doesn't become all work and no play I started to reserve days for friends and family. Note that I don't necessarily know in advance which friend or family member I'm seeing on the days allocated – but these appointments exist in the diary to prevent the time from being swallowed by something else.

When a friend or family member suggests we meet up I find the next *friends and family* day and shuffle my diary accordingly.

At the moment, I reassess the days in my diary once a quarter, and change my diary accordingly. Working on a 'monthly cycle' doesn't seem to work for me. Currently I'm experimenting with a six week cycle.

As you can imagine, my diary looks pretty crowded (you can see an example in a page or two), but it also gives me a level of control over my life that I previously never had. I no longer wonder where the time goes, because I'm the one deciding what time gets spent on what – in advance.

One word of warning – if you decide to run your diary like this be sure to build in some degree of slack - days when there's nothing planned at all. Otherwise it's almost impossible to move things around, and there will always be unexpected appointments that need to be slotted in somehow.

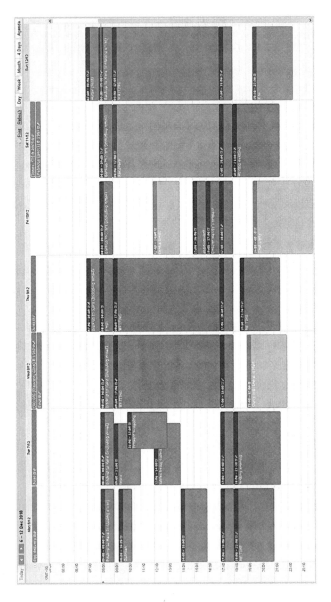

EXHIBIT C: A PAGE FROM MY 'SCARY' DIARY

PUT EVERYTHING ELSE IN YOUR DIARY

Right then - Boxing Day is now in your diary, as well as Now List Day and your Goals Days. Maybe you've also added some extra days of your own creation.

Now it's time to enter everything else – birthdays, anniversaries, appointments, personal holidays, public holidays, reminders, *everything*.

Anything that can use up your valuable time should be in that diary. Flick back to the 'How To Use Your Diary' section early on in this book (or visit the website) for an exhaustive list of time-devouring events.

Move stuff around

If you've done this right there's a good chance you're staring at the most chaotic diary you have ever seen. There are probably clashes and overlapping appointments everywhere! But don't panic. Relax. Crack those knuckles and get ready to play god with your life.

Starting with 'today' and moving as far forward as you feel the need (a couple of weeks works for me), move the appointments around until you've eliminated all the clashes. Don't start cancelling things – that defeats the point of the exercise. But if there's a Boxing Day right on top of your optician's appointment, *move* Boxing Day to a spare slot. If you have working days taking place at the weekend, find an appointment you'd rather do at the weekend and *swap* them.

After a little practice you'll find that you get quite good at this. And it goes without saying that all of this is a LOT easier if you can see a whole week at a time and your diary is electronic.

If you find it's impossible to make everything fit then you may have to go back to the previous stage. This happens to me all the time and is never easy to do.

The diary shuffling exercise isn't a one off task, it's an ongoing process. This isn't a sign that things aren't working – quite the reverse. This is how the process should work.

You might also discover that it's rare to be able to add a new appointment without creating a clash. Again, this isn't a problem. This shows that your time is *valuable* and that you need to decide what it's spent on, rather than giving it away.

Start living by the diary

Now that your diary is planned start living by it day to day. Get into the habit of checking, each morning, or the night before, what you have planned for the next 24 hours. This'll take some getting used to – particularly if you're the sort of person who currently gets out of bed, or arrives at work, and basically does whatever comes to hand.

Now that you're letting the diary dictate how you're spending your time you may notice that it's not as easy to say 'yes' when someone asks if you can make a meeting or if you can spare some time to help them out. Again, that's evidence that the diary is working its magic. Agree to help or meet that person if you want to, but only if you can fit them into your busy schedule.

One final diary tip. Nobody else has to know what's in your diary. In my experience showing people your diary is never a good idea. It merely opens a discussion about what you've chosen to spend your time on, and you'll probably find that people who want a piece of you rarely feel as passionately about your need for a Boxing Day as you do. Keep your diary - or portions of it - private.

A Day in the Life of You

So ... you've made lists, and you've organised your time. I thought it might be quite helpful to finish up with examples of how three of your 'Days' might look, using my life as a example.

Boxing Day

The following is an entry from my Boxing Day journal. (Yes, I keep a Boxing Day journal[30]! So sue me!) This particular Boxing Day followed the last night performance of 'The Importance of Being Earnest'[31]:

> ➤ Got up a little later than usual. Boxing Day initially cancelled because a friend wanted to be picked up from the airport so I swapped it for a half day Now List day. By 9:40am I'd made treacle tart (which was on the Now List). Felt good.
> ➤ My friend cancelled the airport pickup (!!) so elected to have Boxing Day after all.
> ➤ Checked emails and spent some time on Facebook downloading the cast photos.
> ➤ Resized partitions to make more space on my 'music' drive.

---

[30] Just to be clear, I'm not suggesting for one moment that you should keep a Boxing Day journal of your own. I only started it recently as part of an ongoing self-experiment – you know what I'm like.
[31] Which, if you've been paying close attention, you'll remember was on my Now List

- I ate two slices of treacle tart whilst watching the movie The Importance of Being Earnest – this was a great idea. Thoroughly enjoyed the film knowing all I now know about the play. Tart was a little stodgy.
- After the movie called Mum to discuss the tart.
- Did a little writing – didn't really mean to, just started reading the chapters by my bed, then making notes, then before I'd known it I'd ticked off three items on my writing to-do list.
- Had a walk to the shops. Bought stuff to make pizza.
- Sorted through all my old LPs and singles, making a list of the ones I haven't got on my iPod. Then I went and downloaded them all from the Amazon MP3 store and sent a text to Ellen to tell her I had three boxes of records she could have for her vinyl collection. She was chuffed to bits.
- Long relaxing bath
- Made pizza – from scratch! Base included!
- Decided to watch another movie. Pizza was amazing. Movie was total trash.
- By 9:30pm I was utterly booshed. Went to bed and listened to audio book for well over an hour.
- Early night.

Now List Day

My Now List Days are only ever a full day if I'm doing something off the list. Otherwise they're half days. This is what my last Now List (Half) Day looked like:

Now List Item: Go to a 'Pop-up' Restaurant
Researched restaurants on the internet and signed up for a
couple of mailing lists.

Now List Item: Games Evening
Asked around and couldn't get a consensus from my friends
as to when would be a good time to host a games evening.
Everyone is so busy between now and Christmas. Decided to
move this to the Time Sensitive portion of the list and to try
again in the New Year.

Now List Item: See Bill Bailey
Visited the Bill Bailey site. Again. Discovered Bill Bailey is
finally back in the UK and performing at the Wyndham in the
West End. Only a few tickets left. Booked two.

Now List Item: See Imogen Heap
Only a month to go before I go and see Imogen Heap at the
Albert Hall. Emailed friends to see who would like to go with
me.

And that was it! Half day over. You might think I didn't
really achieve very much but from my perspective I nudged
four items from my Now List forward[32].

Goals Day

I split my Goals Day into two and work one goal in the
morning, and another goal in the afternoon. I decide on the

---

[32] And by the way, both Bill and Imogen were fabulous.

day itself which of my three goals I work on, depending on which of the two I want most at that given moment.

Today is a Goals Day.

This morning was spent working on the website that accompanies my novel, whilst this afternoon has been spent finishing this very section!

And am I going to achieve my goal of having this book on shelves before the end of 2010?

No.

Not a chance.

There are only a few more days before Christmas, and before this book is anywhere near ready there's a mountain of editing and proofreading and formatting to do.

But I will get there. You know I will.

After all, you're reading it now, aren't you?

You Still Here?

And there was me, thinking that last page would drive you from your armchair in a frenzy of goal setting. Ah, but I can see from the smile on your face that you have no intention of doing so, that today is a day for doing whatever you feel like. Tell me, is it Boxing Day?

And whilst we're on the subject, how's your Now List coming along? When was the last time you created a memory?

I got an email today from a feller that owns a fishing boat. He's agreed to take me on a trip – I'm finally going see my house from the estuary! And next week I'm off to Rome with Denny.

Final Remarks

If you learn nothing else from this book, remember this – you have only a finite number of days on this earth, and they may be less than you think. A lot less. Why would you want to spend one moment longer than you have to, being less than happy?

The American President John F. Kennedy allegedly told this tale about the great French Marshall Lyautey who once asked his gardener to plant a tree; the gardener objected, saying that the tree was 'slow growing' and would not reach maturity for 100 years. The Marshall replied, "In that case, my dear man, there is no time to lose; plant it this afternoon!"

Boxing Days, Now Lists, Wishes and Goals. They're very different trees. But oh, what fruit. Go on, plant yourself a forest.

Best wishes, Peter

Acknowledgements

Well this is exciting, I've never had to write an acknowledgements section before. It's a little like standing on the podium at an awards ceremony, only without an award, or the applause, or the dinner jackets. Ok, so it's nothing like an awards ceremony. It's more like standing on a street corner shouting at anyone who happens to be walking past - and that's a shame, because there's a small, select group of people without whom I could have never have got this book 'out there', and they really deserve the 'awards ceremony' style of acknowledgement. So if you could just imagine the lights, the cameras, the glasses of champagne – I'd very much appreciate it.

In no particular order I'd really like to thank:

My totally fabulous and long-suffering assistant, Jules – for making the really important stuff in my life 'happen', listening to my endless babble and nonsense, reading my 'stuff' (several times, even when it was total rubbish), and generally putting up with me. I couldn't have done this without you.

My dear friend Wendy – my 'wise and sexy guru' - for her endless passion, advice and encouragement, for reminding me that there's more to life than we can see with our eyes or hear with our ears, whilst at the same time keeping my feet on the ground. But most of all for keeping me on track, focused, and believing in me when I wasn't so sure.

Alison the Proof Fairy - for stamping out all my stupid grammatical errors and without whom people would question my ability to string two words together (you can find her at theprooffairy.com).

Agent Sparkles - for her fabulous thoughts and ideas, particularly about General Unhappiness, but also throughout. Anne and Denny - for being hugely influential in the 'Goals' section of this book.

Ellen for her fabulous cover design & artwork. Find out more about her at www.an-occasional-dream.com

Gaynor at authorsonline.co.uk for all her advice.

Simon Whalley and the other authors and tutors at Swanwick 2010, for showing me a way forward.

And my 'First Readers'; Lucy, Lucy, Patrick and Karen – for their invaluable comments, thoughts, feedback, support and encouragement.

Thank you all.

About the Author

 Peter Jones started life as a particularly rubbish Graphic Designer, followed by a stint as a mediocre Petrol Pump Attendant. After that he got embroiled in the murky world of credit cards until a freak accident with a zip zap machine (remember those?) restructured his DNA at the molecular level and gave him entrepreneurial powers. Now, when Peter's not filling his days with the things he laughably calls work, he's writing. Even as we speak he's finishing up his debut novel, snappily entitled "The Good Guy's Guide to Getting Girls". It's good stuff. Honest. But don't take our word for it, read more at: www.thegoodguysguidetogettinggirls.com

Peter lives just a few miles outside London with his cat CJ, who's possibly the smartest animal never to have appeared in a cartoon. From his window he can see France and the Eiffel Tower. Or is that Canvey Island Oil Refinery?

He doesn't own a large departmental store and probably isn't the same guy you've seen on the TV show Dragons' Den.

You can find out more about Peter Jones, his "How To Do Everything And Be Happy" seminars, and the subjects raised in this book at www.howtodoeverythingandbehappy.com

Coming Soon

What do you do when all the single women have disappeared and internet dating has yet to be invented?
Get creative.

Boxing Day, 1997, and Jason Smith, 29 and self-confessed good guy, is single again. But now that he's free it seems the sexy single girls - the "Melanies" of this world - are in short supply.

Or are they? Has Jason stumbled on a foolproof way to bring girls right to his front door?

Both aided and hindered by his beer-drinking best buddy and reluctant father-to-be Alex, his ever-wise, ever-sarcastic colleague Sian, his arch nemesis and local lothario Gary, and his ever faithful Kylie calendar, Jason throws himself into parties, dating and cookery classes and eventually settles on glamour photography as a ruse to find his "perfect woman."

Appealing to fans of Mike Gayle and Nick Hornby, Peter Jones's "Good Guy's Guide to Getting Girls" follows Jason on a voyage of self-discovery as he experiences the pitfalls of being a glamour photographer and the highs and lows of trying to meet one's soul mate at the turn of the millennium.

Find out more at
www.thegoodguysguidetogettinggirls.com

Lightning Source UK Ltd.
Milton Keynes UK
UKOW050758150312

189028UK00001B/26/P